UNIT ONE

UNIT
ONE

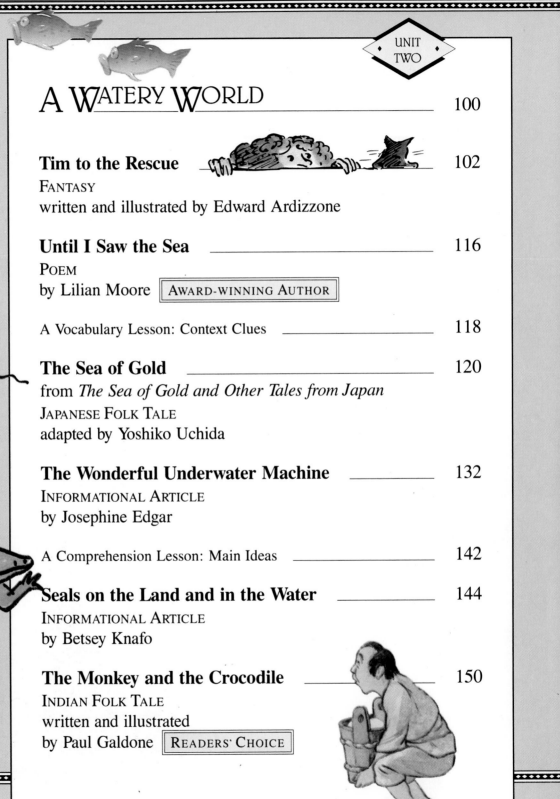

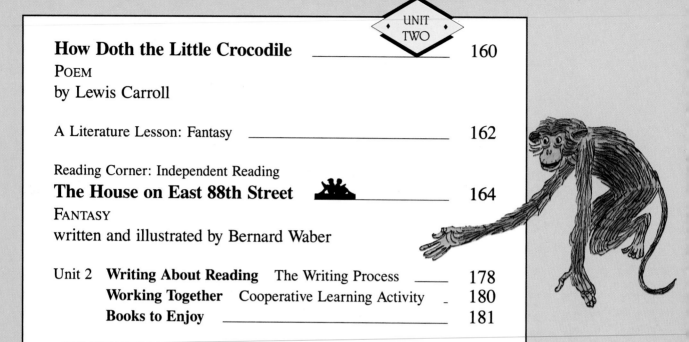
UNIT
TWO

9

Get the Message 250

REMEMBER WHEN...

*R*eading can help us learn about the past.

What events from the past are worth remembering?

detail of SNAP THE WHIP,
*oil on canvas by Winslow Homer,
American, 1872*

When I Was Nine

written and illustrated by James Stevenson

The author of this story tells about a special time when he was about your age.

My own children are grown up now; that's how old I am. But sometimes I look back and I remember. . . .

When I was nine, we lived on a street with big trees.

I had a bicycle, and I knew where all the bumps were on the sidewalk.

We had a dog named Jocko.

Our telephone looked like this.
Our number was 3348.

My father had boots and a
bugle from when he was in the
army in the First World War, and a mandolin
from when he was in school. Sometimes
when he came home from work, he would
play taps for us.

At night our mother would read to us.

We lived near a railroad. Before I went to sleep, I listened to the steam locomotives. The freight trains and the express trains blew their whistles as they went racketing by in the dark.

In our backyard there was a beech tree. If you climbed high enough, you could see the Hudson River and smoke from the trains.

After school I listened to the radio and did homework. (There was no television.)

Bill, who lived next door, was my best friend. He was ten. Bill was pretty good fun, but only about half the time.

When my brother had a friend over, they wouldn't let me play. I learned to pitch by throwing a ball against the garage door.

I put out a weekly newspaper. I collected news from all the people on our block.

DID ANYTHING HAPPEN THIS WEEK?

No.

HOW I PRINTED THE NEIGHBORHOOD NEWS

1. I TOOK A CAN OF HEKTOGRAPH AND OPENED IT. HEKTOGRAPH WAS LIKE A THICK JELLY SOUP.

2. I DUMPED IT INTO A SAUCEPAN AND HEATED IT ON THE STOVE,

3. THEN POURED IT INTO A PAN AND LET IT COOL AND HARDEN.

4. MEANWHILE, I WROTE THE PAPER WITH A SPECIAL PURPLE PENCIL.

5. THEN I PUT THAT PAPER FACE-DOWN ON THE HARD JELLY AND RUBBED IT SMOOTH.

6. WHEN I PULLED OFF THE PAPER---

(7.) --- THE <u>NEIGHBORHOOD</u> <u>NEWS</u> WAS WRITTEN ON THE JELLY BACKWARDS!

(8.) THEN I PUT A CLEAN SHEET OF PAPER ON IT AND RUBBED, AND I GOT A COPY OF THE <u>NEWS</u>. I COULD MAKE LOTS OF COPIES.

Not everybody wanted one.

MR. FINERTY, WOULD YOU LIKE TO BUY A COPY OF <u>THE NEIGHBORHOOD NEWS</u>?

NOT RIGHT NOW.

Most summers my brother and I went to visit our grandmother, who had a house near the beach. We went swimming every day.

Grandma was a lot of fun. We would crawl into her room in the morning and hide under her bed.

Then we would pretend to be a funny radio program; she always acted surprised and she always laughed.

But this summer was different. In July we packed up the car for a trip out west. A neighbor said he would take care of Jocko. Bill and Tony waved goodbye.

We drove for days and days. My brother and I argued a lot. When it got too bad, our father stopped the car and made us throw a football for a while. Then we got back in the car again.

At the end of each day we looked for a place to stay. "What do we think?" my father would say.

"Plenty good enough," my mother would say. And we would stop for the night.

My brother and I always wanted to stop and see something special. Our parents usually wanted to keep going. "Too many tourists," they said. But in Missouri we visited a big cave.

Our parents woke us up one night to look at the sky. "What's happening?" I asked. The sky was shimmering.

"It's the Northern Lights," said my mother.

On my birthday we stopped in a small town and went into a store. My parents bought me exactly what I always wanted . . . a cowboy hat.

At last we came to New Mexico.

We stayed at a ranch and went on long, hot rides into the mountains.

One day we rode to a waterfall. While the horses rested, we slid down the waterfall and plunged into an icy pool. We did it again and again.

It was the most fun I'd ever had.

We drove back home in August. As we turned into our block, Jocko ran to greet us. It was great to get home.

Everything looked just the way it always had . . . except maybe a little smaller.

But I was probably a little bigger. I wasn't nine any more.

◆ LIBRARY LINK ◆

If you liked this story by James Stevenson, you might enjoy reading another of his books, Howard.

Reader's Response

Do you think you would have liked the trip to New Mexico as much as the author did? Why or why not?

When I Was Nine

Questions

1. Why wasn't there a television set in the author's house?
2. How did the summer when the author was nine compare to other summers?
3. What were some of the sights the family saw on the way to New Mexico?
4. How can you tell that the author liked his grandmother?
5. Was the author happy when he was a boy? How do you know?

Writing to Learn

THINK AND PREDICT   Mr. Stevenson writes about a special year of his childhood. When you are grown up, what do you think you will remember about this year of your life? Read Mr. Stevenson's list. Then write your own list.

Things Mr. Stevenson Remembered	Things I Will Remember About This Year
• Dad had a bugle. • Mother read to us. • I put out a newspaper.	(Make your list.)

WRITE   Read your list. Circle your favorite memory. Write sentences to tell what you will remember about this year when you grow up.

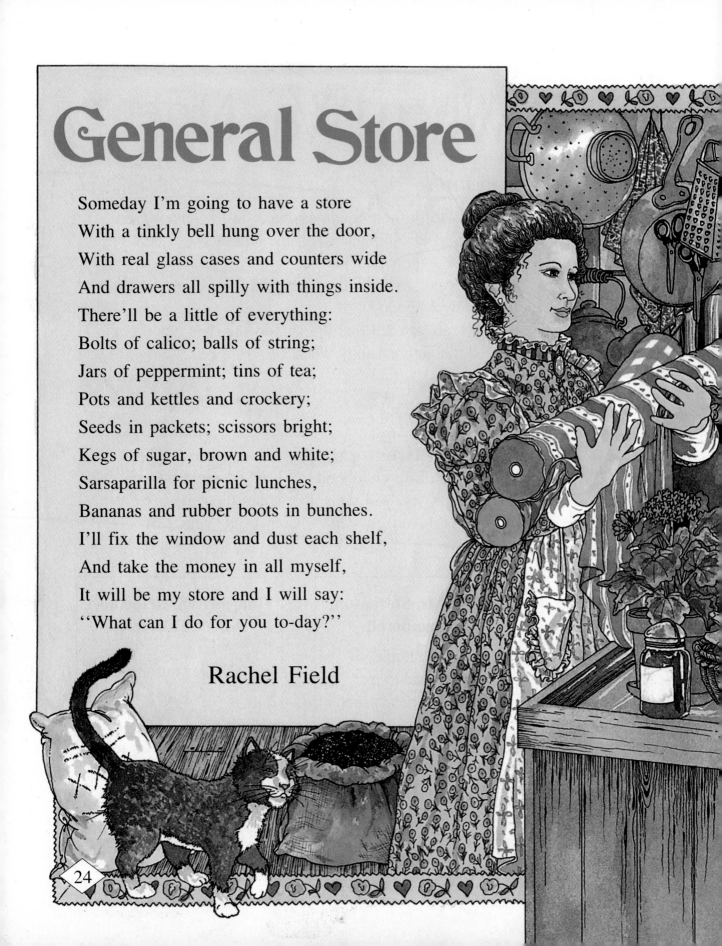

General Store

Someday I'm going to have a store
With a tinkly bell hung over the door,
With real glass cases and counters wide
And drawers all spilly with things inside.
There'll be a little of everything:
Bolts of calico; balls of string;
Jars of peppermint; tins of tea;
Pots and kettles and crockery;
Seeds in packets; scissors bright;
Kegs of sugar, brown and white;
Sarsaparilla for picnic lunches,
Bananas and rubber boots in bunches.
I'll fix the window and dust each shelf,
And take the money in all myself,
It will be my store and I will say:
"What can I do for you to-day?"

Rachel Field

Grateful acknowledgment is made to the following publishers, authors, and agents for their permission to reprint copyrighted material. Any adaptations are noted in the individual acknowledgments and are made with the full knowledge and approval of the authors or their representatives. Every effort has been made to locate all copyright proprietors; any errors or omissions in copyright notice are inadvertent and will be corrected in future printings as they are discovered.

Alexander and the Terrible, Horrible, No Good, Very Bad Day by Judith Viorst and illustrated by Ray Cruz. Text copyright © 1972 by Judith Viorst. Pictures copyright © 1972 by Ray Cruz. Reprinted by permission of the American publisher, Macmillan Publishing Company, of the British publisher, Angus & Robertson (UK), and of the author's agents, Lescher & Lescher, Ltd.

"The Boy Who Cried Wolf" adapted by Genie Iverson, © 1989 by Genie Iverson.

"A Day When Frogs Wear Shoes" adapted from *More Stories Julian Tells* by Ann Cameron, illustrated by Ann Strugnell. Copyright © 1986 by Ann Cameron. Illustrations copyright © 1986 by Ann Strugnell. Reprinted by permission of the American publisher, Alfred A. Knopf, Inc., and of the British publisher, Victor Gollancz Ltd.

Forecast by Malcolm Hall, illustrated by Bruce Degen. Text copyright © 1977 by Malcolm Hall, illustrations © 1977 by Bruce Degen. Adapted and reprinted by permission of Coward, McCann & Geoghegan.

"General Store" from *Taxis and Toadstools* by Rachel Field. Copyright 1926 by Rachel Field. Reprinted by permission of the American publisher, Doubleday, a division of Bantam, Doubleday, Dell Publishing Group, Inc., and of the British publisher, William Heinemann Ltd.

Acknowledgments continue on pages 382–384, which constitute an extension of this copyright page.

CASTLES
OF
·SAND·

WORLD OF READING

CASTLES OF SAND

P. David Pearson   Dale D. Johnson

Theodore Clymer   Roselmina Indrisano   Richard L. Venezky

James F. Baumann   Elfrieda Hiebert   Marian Toth

Consulting Authors

Carl Grant   Jeanne Paratore

SILVER BURDETT & GINN

NEEDHAM, MA • MORRISTOWN, NJ
ATLANTA, GA • CINCINNATI, OH • DALLAS, TX
MENLO PARK, CA • NORTHFIELD, IL

Phillis Wheatley
America's First Black Poet

Questions

1. How did Phillis Wheatley come to America?
2. What was special about the way in which the Wheatleys treated Phillis?
3. How did learning to read and write change Phillis Wheatley's life?
4. Do you think Phillis Wheatley's life was unusual? What led you to your answer?

Writing to Learn

THINK AND DESCRIBE   Can you make a character map of Phillis Wheatley? Think about what she was like and the things she did. Then, on your paper, complete the character map of her.

Phillis had a will to learn.

_____

_____

_____

_____

Phillis Wheatley

WRITE   Write sentences that tell what kind of person Phillis Wheatley was.

233

Study Skill:

Parts of a Book

A Day When Frogs Wear Shoes" is just one of many stories in Ann Cameron's book *More Stories Julian Tells*. Finding a story or a chapter—as well as other information—in a book is easy if you know the parts of a book. These parts include the title page, copyright page, table of contents, glossary, and index.

When you open a book, one of the first pages you see is the title page. This page tells you the title of the book and the name of its author. If the book is illustrated, the artist's name usually appears as well. The title page also gives the name and location of the book's publisher. Look at the title page from *More Stories Julian Tells*. Who published the book?

The copyright page comes right after the title page. Look at the copyright page from *More Stories Julian Tells*. It tells you the year the book was published.

> **More
> Stories Julian Tells**
>
> by ANN CAMERON
> Illustrated by Ann Strugnell
>
> ALFRED A. KNOPF • NEW YORK

> This is a Borzoi Book
> published by Alfred A. Knopf, Inc.
>
> Text copyright
> © 1986 by Ann Cameron
> Illustrations copyright
> © 1986 by Ann Strugnell

You will also find a table of contents at the front of a book that has more than one story or chapter. Look at the table of contents on the right. Next to each story is the page number on which the story begins.

Many books also have useful information at the back of the book. Some books have a list at the back of difficult words and their meanings. The words are listed in alphabetical order. This list is called a glossary.

Some books have an index at the back. An index tells you where to find specific information in a book. The information is always arranged in alphabetical order. Suppose you wanted to read about frogs in your science textbook. You would look in the index under *F.* Then find the word *frog.* The index will tell you what page or pages have information about frogs.

Contents

Using What You Have Learned

1. Find the table of contents in this textbook. List three stories or poems that you especially liked. Next to each title, write the page on which the story or poem begins.
2. When was the book *More Stories Julian Tells* published?
3. Which story in the book is the longest?

Literature:

Repetition

What story do these words come from?

"I'll huff and I'll puff and I'll blow your house in."

They are from "The Three Little Pigs." The wolf repeats them in exactly the same way each time he tries to get into the houses of the little pigs. The repeated use of a phrase, a word, or a sound is called repetition.

In "The Little Red Hen" these words are repeated again and again:

"Not I," said the duck.
"Not I," said the cat.
"Not I," said the dog.
"Then I will," said the Little Red Hen.
And she did.

Why do we like stories with repetition? One reason is that they are easy to remember. We don't have to hear much of "The Little Red Hen" before we can join the storyteller on the parts that are repeated. And when the wolf comes to the next little pig's house, we know exactly what he will call out. So repetition also helps us guess what will happen next in a story.

Another reason for liking stories with repetition is that repeated words and sounds are fun. They tickle our ears. In "The House on East 88th Street," you may have laughed when you read "swish, swash, splash, swoosh" for the third and fourth times. The words just sound funny when they are said.

More Uses of Repetition

Read the following part of the poem "Try, Try Again" to see how the poet uses repetition.

> Try, try again
> 'Tis a lesson you should heed
> Try, try again
> If at first you don't succeed
> Try, try again . . . .

Poetry often uses repetition. The line "Try, try again" gives the poem rhythm. It also helps the poet make his point. He keeps repeating his words just as he wants us to repeat our efforts to succeed.

Read and Enjoy

When you read the next story, "Alexander and the Terrible, Horrible, No Good, Very Bad Day," you will see again how repetition can be funny. See if you can guess when something is going to be repeated.

Alexander

Horrible, No Good,

and the Terrible, Very Bad Day

written by Judith Viorst
illustrated by Ray Cruz

We all have days when everything seems to go wrong. But wait until you hear what happens to Alexander!

I went to sleep with gum in my mouth and now there's gum in my hair and when I got out of bed this morning I tripped on the skateboard and by mistake I dropped my sweater in the sink while the water was running and I could tell it was going to be a terrible, horrible, no good, very bad day.

At breakfast Anthony found a Corvette Sting Ray car kit in his breakfast cereal box and Nick found a Junior Undercover Agent code ring in his breakfast cereal box but in my breakfast cereal box all I found was breakfast cereal.

I think I'll move to Australia.

In the car pool Mrs. Gibson let Becky have a seat by the window. Audrey and Elliott got seats by the window too. I said I was being scrunched. I said I was being smushed. I said, if I don't get a seat by the window I am going to be carsick. No one even answered.

I could tell it was going to be a terrible, horrible, no good, very bad day.

At school Mrs. Dickens liked Paul's picture of the sailboat better than my picture of the invisible castle.

At singing time she said I sang too loud. At counting time she said I left out sixteen. Who needs sixteen?

I could tell it was going to be a terrible, horrible, no good, very bad day.

I could tell because Paul said I wasn't his best friend anymore. He said that Philip Parker was his best friend and that Albert Moyo was his next best friend and that I was only his third best friend.

I hope you sit on a tack, I said to Paul. I hope the next time you get a double-decker strawberry ice-cream cone the ice cream part falls off the cone part and lands in Australia.

There were two cupcakes in Philip Parker's lunch bag and Albert got a Hershey bar with almonds and Paul's mother gave him a piece of jelly roll that had little coconut sprinkles on the top. Guess whose mother forgot to put in dessert?

It was a terrible, horrible, no good, very bad day.

That's what it was, because after school my mom took us all to the dentist and Dr. Fields found a cavity just in me. Come back next week and I'll fix it, said Dr. Fields.

Next week, I said, I'm going to Australia.

On the way downstairs the elevator door closed on my foot and while we were waiting for my mom to go get the car Anthony made me fall where it was muddy and then when I started crying because of the mud Nick said I was a crybaby and while I was punching Nick for saying crybaby my Mom came back with the car and scolded me for being muddy and fighting.

I am having a terrible, horrible, no good, very bad day, I told everybody. No one even answered.

So we went to the shoestore to buy some sneakers. Anthony chose white ones with blue stripes. Nick chose red ones with white stripes. I chose blue ones with red stripes but then the shoe man said, We're all sold out. They made me buy plain old white ones, but they can't make me wear them.

When we picked up my dad at his office he said
I couldn't play with his copying machine, but I forgot.
He also said to watch out for the books on his desk,
and I was careful as could be except for my elbow.
He also said don't fool around with his phone, but I
think I called Australia. My dad said please don't pick
him up anymore.

It was a terrible, horrible, no good, very bad day.

There were lima beans for dinner and I hate limas.

There was kissing on TV and I hate kissing.

My bath was too hot, I got soap in my eyes, my marble went down the drain, and I had to wear my railroad-train pajamas. I hate my railroad-train pajamas.

When I went to bed Nick took back the pillow he said I could keep and the Mickey Mouse night light burned out and I bit my tongue.

The cat wants to sleep with Anthony, not with me.

It has been a terrible, horrible, no good, very bad day.

My mom says some days are like that.

Even in Australia.

 ◆ LIBRARY LINK ◆

If you enjoyed this story by Judith Viorst, you might enjoy reading another of her stories, If I Were In Charge of the World and Other Worries.

◆ Reader's Response

Do you think that Alexander really wanted to move to Australia? Have you ever felt the way he did? Explain your answers.

WRITING
ABOUT
READING

Writing a Helpful Note

Many of the characters that you read about in this unit had problems to solve. For example, Maria was nervous about her recital. Her sister found a way to help her.

Imagine that you are able to help a character from one of the stories in this unit. What could you do to help? You can write a note telling what you would do.

Prewriting

Choose a story character from this unit whose problem is interesting to you. Reread the story in which that character appears. Think about what you could do to help. This diagram may help you plan.

Helping Hands	
Name of Character	
Character's Problem	
What I Might Do To Help	

Writing

Begin your note with a greeting such as ''Dear Julian.'' Explain to the character your view of the problem. Then write what you could do to help. Tell as clearly as you can *how* you would put your idea into action. Explain why you think you have a good idea.

Revising

Read your note to a partner. Ask your partner if you have explained your ideas clearly. Be sure that all the words tell exactly what you mean. If some words don't, think of other words that explain your ideas more clearly.

Proofreading

Use a dictionary to check your spelling. Make sure you have used periods and commas correctly. Then make a clean copy of your note.

Publishing

Use the notes to create a class newspaper column called ''Helping Hands.''

Making a Story Mobile

Lemonade, a hot sun, frogs, and shoes are all part of the story "A Day When Frogs Wear Shoes."

Today, you and your classmates will make a mobile about a story in this unit.

Before you begin, decide who will be responsible for one or more of these jobs:

◆ Encouraging everyone to share ideas

◆ Making sure everyone understands the directions

◆ Showing appreciation for people's ideas

◆ Recording everyone's ideas on a list

Start by asking someone in the group to gather the materials you will need. Then, together discuss the stories in this unit and choose one for your mobile. Take turns suggesting objects that are important in the story. Make a list of everyone's ideas. Next, each person will draw one of the objects and cut it out. Finally, everyone will help put the mobile together by hanging the pictures from a stick or hanger.

Ask your friends to guess which story your mobile is about.

The Courage of Sarah Noble by Alice Dalgliesh *(Scribner, 1952)* In 1707, a girl helps her father build a log house in the wilderness. When her father sets off to get the rest of the family, Sarah is left to deal with the wilderness alone.

Anna, Grandpa, and the Big Storm by Carla Stevens *(Houghton Mifflin, 1982)* During the great blizzard of 1888 in New York City, Anna is determined to go to the final round of the spelling bee. Grandpa offers to go with her.

Chin Chiang and the Dragon's Dance by Ian Wallace *(Atheneum, 1984)* A young boy is old enough to do the New Year's good luck dance. He is afraid he will be clumsy but finds the courage to try.

GET THE
MESSAGE

*T*alking, writing,
signaling, signing –
why do people
send their
messages in
different ways?

THE LETTER,
painting by Mary Cassatt, American, 1891

*Some people think predicting
the weather is a tough job. Others
think it's a guessing game.*

FORECAST

written by Malcolm Hall
illustrated by Bruce Degen

"Speech! Speech!" the animals chanted.
Theodore Cat smiled and stood up.

"Well, if you insist," he said.

"We didn't mean *you,* Theodore," groaned
the animals. "We want a speech from Stan!"

"Oh, *him*," said Theodore.

Stan Groundhog stood up. The
whole party was in his honor. After
twenty years, Stan was retiring. He was
leaving his job as weather forecaster for
the *Claws and Paws* newspaper. "I can't
think of anything to say," said Stan.

"Then make a forecast!" yelled
Humphrey Snake from the back of
the room.

"What a good idea," said Theodore, who was the editor of the paper and the boss of all the animals. "Stan, give us your last official weather prediction."

"Well—okay," said Stan. He went to the window and peeked outside; next he looked down at his shadow, then he sighed. "I predict it will be warm and sunny all afternoon. There is no chance of rain." The animals cheered. "Now I have to be going," said Stan. "Thanks for the party."

Stan put on a raincoat and galoshes. He opened an umbrella.

"Wait a minute," said Oscar Raccoon. "Why are you going out dressed like that? I thought you said it wasn't going to rain."

"If I have learned one thing," said Stan, "it is never take chances."

And with that, a tremendous crack of lightning jumped across the sky! All the lights in the office went out. Rain began to pour down.

"Do you see what I mean?" said Stan. He waved good-bye and left.

The lights flickered a bit and finally came back on. Oscar looked around. "Is everybody okay?" One by one, the animals nodded. Except— where was Theodore? "Theodore!" shouted Oscar. "Where are you?"

"There he is!" shouted Frank Beaver. He pointed to the floor. "I see his tail!"

Theodore's face was red as he crawled out from under the desk. The animals grinned. "I wasn't hiding, if that's what you're all thinking," he snapped. "I was—uh—considering something—that's what I was doing."

"Oh? And what were you considering?" asked Oscar.

Theodore glared. "I was considering that we will need a new forecaster to take Stan's place. So there!" Theodore looked around the room. "Does anyone know a groundhog who needs a job?"

Caroline Porcupine raised her hand. "Does the forecaster *have* to be a groundhog?"

"Of course," said Theodore. "Everyone knows that groundhogs know *whether* or not spring is coming. That's why they make good *whethermen.*"

Caroline went on. "Anyway, Theodore," she said, "I want the job, even if I am not a groundhog. I know a lot about the weather. Last year, I took a class in meteorology."

"Meteorology?" said Humphrey. "What's that mean?"

"Meteorology is the science of weather," said Caroline. "I can make real forecasts—not just guesses like Stan. If you give me a chance, I will prove it."

"Okay," grumbled Theodore. "Let's make a bet. You forecast the weather for all next week. If you are right five days in a row, I will *consider* you for the job. But if you are wrong once, I'll get a groundhog."

"Theodore, I'll take your bet," said Caroline.

The next day, Caroline brought in her weather instruments. All that morning, Caroline set them up. Soon wires and dials were everywhere.

By afternoon she was ready. She looked at the instruments, one after the other. On a pad of paper she wrote down how hot it was, how damp it was, how fast the wind was blowing, and everything else.

Then Caroline picked up the telephone. She called forecasters all over the country. They told her what the weather was like in their towns. Caroline wrote this down, too.

Finally, Caroline put all the numbers on a map. She connected the numbers with lines. Just then Theodore walked up. "Very good," he said. "I have never seen a better drawing of spaghetti!" He laughed and laughed at his own joke.

Caroline looked up. "I am ready to make my forecast. Today is Monday. It will be clear for the rest of the day. Tuesday, it will be sunny and warm. Wednesday, it will be windy and cold. Thursday, it will rain."

The animals looked at each other and smiled. So far, the forecast sounded good— maybe Caroline would be right!

Caroline went on. "And last, Friday. It will be cold in the morning, with snow in the afternoon."

Theodore yeowled with laughter. "Snow? Did you say *snow*? Caroline, look outside. It's the middle of summer!"

Caroline folded her arms stubbornly across her chest. "My instruments say it will snow on Friday. Anyway, every now and then it does snow in summer. In July of 1816, for example . . ."

"Okay, okay," said Theodore. "If it snows on Friday, you get the job for sure. But meanwhile, I'm going to keep on looking for a groundhog!"

That afternoon was sunny. The day after that was warm and clear. Caroline had been right.

Wednesday was windy and cold. Caroline had been right again. Everyone clapped her on the back. Except Theodore. He stared gloomily out his window. "She has been right three days in a row," he thought. "That is better than Stan ever did."

Thursday started out rainy and stayed that way the whole day. Theodore tromped in, soaked, as mad and miserable as a wet cat. Again, he thought. "Four days in a row. Maybe I *should* give Caroline the job even if it doesn't snow on Friday."

But then—"Aaaaa—choooo!" Theodore sneezed. Papers flew everywhere.

"Now see what's happened," he snarled. "I have a cold. And it's all Caroline's fault! If she hadn't forecast this rain, it never would have happened!"

That night, Frank and Oscar walked home together. "It's too bad Caroline predicted snow," said Frank. "She really wants that job."

Oscar nodded. "It will never snow tomorrow. Poor Caroline." Then Oscar stopped. He winked at Frank. "Suppose we help the weather a bit? Even if it only snowed a little, Theodore would still have to give Caroline the job."

"What do you have in mind?" asked Frank.

"Come to my house for dinner," said Oscar, "and I will tell you."

Friday started out cold, just as Caroline had predicted. But by noon, there was still no sign of snow. Theodore sat in his office sniffling and looking out the window.

If Theodore had turned his head, he would have seen Frank and Oscar tiptoe past his door. Each one carried a large sack. They were headed for the ladder that went up to the roof.

A few minutes later, Theodore gasped. A white flake had drifted down past his window! Then came another flake . . . and another . . . and another! He jumped up. "Snow! It's really snowing!"

Theodore ran out of his office. "Caroline! Congratulations! It's snowing! You are the greatest forecaster ever! I take back everything I said."

Theodore was so excited, he nearly hugged Caroline. He remembered just in time that you *never* hug a porcupine.

So instead he dragged Caroline into his office. "See!" He pointed outside at the flakes.

Caroline squinted. "That doesn't look like snow to me," she said.

"Of course it is," said Theodore. He raised the window. Flakes started to drift in. One landed on Theodore's nose. "*Aaaa—choo*!!!" For a moment Theodore looked surprised. Then, he looked suspicious.

"Snow never tickled before. Let me see that
'snowflake.'" He grabbed the flake. "I thought
so. This is a *feather*!"

Theodore ran to the window. He poked his
head outside and looked up at the roof. There
was Oscar, holding a half-empty pillowcase in
one hand and a handful of feathers in the other.

"Come down from there!" roared Theodore.

A few minutes later, Oscar and Caroline
were standing side by side in Theodore's office.
"So! You two thought you could trick me."

"Caroline had nothing to do with this," said
Oscar. "It was all my idea."

"Hah!" Theodore snorted. "I don't believe you, any more than I really believed it was snowing out there." He pointed out the window. Once more, flakes were drifting down.

"What? More feathers? That does it! I suppose Frank's up there, too."

Again Theodore poked his head out the window. But this time, it was *really* snowing. A large, powdery snowball whacked him between the eyes!

"*Whaaag!*" spat Theodore. Then he licked his whiskers. "That's *real* snow!"

"Of course it is," said Caroline. "I told you it would snow."

Just then, Frank came climbing down the ladder from the roof. His brown fur was covered with snow. "Theodore! Caroline! Oscar! Why are you still inside? Come on out!"

And they all did.

◆ LIBRARY LINK ◆

If you liked reading this story by Malcolm Hall, you might enjoy reading another of his books, Headlines.

Reader's Response

Would you try to help a friend the way Oscar and Frank did? Why or why not?

FORECAST

Questions

1. Why were the animals having a party?
2. What did you learn about Theodore when you read he had crawled under his desk?
3. Why did Theodore think that a weather forecaster had to be a groundhog?
4. Why was Caroline confident she could do a good job?
5. Do you think the test Theodore gave Caroline was fair? Why? How did you decide on your answer?

Writing to Learn

THINK AND IMAGINE   Imagine that you are a weather forecaster. Draw a simple outline of the state where you live. Add symbols to show what the weather is like. Use snowflakes, raindrops, a sun, or clouds (with puffy cheeks for wind). Use numbers to show the temperature.

WRITE   Write sentences to describe the weather shown on your map. Is it sunny or cloudy? Is it going to rain or snow? Is it windy? What is the temperature?

Secret Talk

I have a friend
and sometimes we meet
and greet each other
without a word.

We walk through a field
and stalk a bird
and chew a blade of
pungent grass.

We let time pass
for a golden hour
while we twirl a flower
of Queen Anne's lace

or find a lion's face
shaped in a cloud
that's drifting, sifting
across the sky.

There's no need to say,
"It's been a fine day"
when we say goodbye:
when we say goodbye
we just wave a hand
and we understand.

Eve Merriam

265

Words In Our Hands

by Ada B. Litchfield

There are many ways to "talk" and to "listen."

My name is Michael Turner. I am nine years old. I have two sisters, Gina and Diane, a dog named Polly, and two parents who can't hear me when I talk.

They never have heard me. You see, my mom and dad were born deaf.

My parents never heard any sounds at all when they were babies. Some people think a person who can't hear can't learn to talk. That's not true.

My mom and dad went to a school for deaf kids when they were growing up. That's where they learned to talk. They learned by placing their fingers on their teacher's throat and feeling how words felt in her voice box as she said them. They learned how words looked by watching her face, especially her lips, as she spoke. It's hard to learn to say words that way. But my parents did.

They don't talk much now, but they can talk. Their voices are not like other peoples'. My parents have never heard other people talking or even their own voices, so they don't know how voices sound. It's not always easy to understand what they are saying, but Gina and Diane and I can.

Sometimes my mother and father can understand what people are saying by reading their lips. That's another thing my parents learned at their school—lip reading.

Reading lips is hard. Some people don't move their lips much when they talk, or they hide their mouths with their hands. Besides, many words look alike when you say them. Look in the mirror and say *pin* and *bin, hand* and *and*, *hill* and *ill*. See what I mean?

How we move our bodies and what our faces look like when we talk help our parents read our lips. But most of the time we talk to them with our hands as well as our mouths. Grandma Ellis says we have words in our hands.

One way to talk with your hands is to learn a special alphabet so you can spell words with your fingers. This is called finger spelling.

Look at this alphabet. Can you finger spell your name?

Another way to hand talk is to use sign language. Once you have learned sign language, it is easier and faster than finger spelling.

Everybody uses sign language. You can tell your friends to "go away" without using your voice. But sign language for the deaf is like French or Spanish. You have to learn many signs that other people understand before you can talk to anybody.

The International Manual Alphabet

Gina, Diane, and I are learning new signs all the time. My mother and father learned sign language when they were little. They taught us signs when we were babies, just as hearing parents teach their children words. Our grandparents, friends, and neighbors helped us learn to talk.

We are a happy family. At least we were until about six months ago. Then the publishing company where my father has always worked moved to a new town, one hundred miles away.

My father is the editor of a magazine about farming. Nobody in the family wanted to move. But my father loves his job so, of course, he wanted to go with his company.

We moved into a new house with a big yard that everybody liked, but it took a long time to get used to our new town. Before, my mom had always done all the shopping and banking for our family. Now she felt a little strange going into a store or bank where the people didn't know her. Very often she wanted Gina or me to go with her.

In our old town, everybody knew our family. Nobody stared when they saw us talking with our hands. But in the new town, people did stare. Of course, they pretended they didn't see us, but I knew they were looking.

It was even worse when my mom and dad talked. It seemed as if everyone looked at us when they heard my parents' strange-sounding voices. Sometimes Gina and I felt embarrassed, especially when we had to tell someone what my mother or father had said.

Gina and I didn't want to feel that way. We knew how shy our parents felt. We knew they were as lonesome and homesick as we were!

One awful day I saw three kids making fun of my parents. They were standing behind Mom and Dad and pretending to talk with their hands. I was so upset I wanted to pretend something, too. Just for a minute, I wanted to pretend my mother and father were not my parents. I had never felt that way before.

I was really so ashamed of myself.

That very same day Gina's favorite teacher gave her an invitation for our family to go to a performance of the National Theatre of the Deaf.

At first, I didn't want to give the invitation to my parents. I didn't want them to go. I didn't want people to make fun of them or feel sorry for Gina and me.

But Gina said they should go. She said that the play would be in sign language, and who would understand it better than our parents? I knew she was right. Besides, Mom and Dad needed to go out and meet new people.

Still, I was worried about what might happen. The night of the play, all sorts of questions were popping into my mind as I dragged up the steps into the hall. Then I saw those same three kids standing in the doorway. One of them grinned and wiggled his hands at me. That made me angry!

The big hall was filled with people. Just inside the door, my mother signed to me, "Where will we sit?"

To our surprise, a man stood up and said, "There are five seats over here."

We couldn't believe it. He was using sign language!

All around us, people were laughing and talking. Many of them were talking with their hands. They didn't seem to care who was watching.

Before the play started, we learned from our program that some of the actors were deaf and some could hear. The hearing actors and some of the deaf actors would speak in the play. All of the actors would sign, sometimes for themselves and sometimes for each other. Sometimes they would all sign together. Everyone in the audience would be able to understand what was going on.

The play we saw was called *The Wooden Boy*. It was about Pinocchio, a puppet who wanted to be a real boy. It was both funny and sad.

After the play, we went backstage to meet the actors. The deaf performers talked with people who knew sign language. The hearing performers helped the other people understand what was being said.

I was proud of my parents. They were smiling, and their fingers were flying as fast as anyone's. For the first time in many months, they seemed to feel at home.

Then we had another surprise. Gina's teacher came over to us. She talked very slowly and carefully so my mother could read her lips. Then she signed with her hands!

Gina was excited. Her favorite teacher, who wasn't deaf, had words in her hands, too. Gina was learning something she didn't know before. We all were. We were learning there were many friendly people in our new town who could talk with our parents. I decided this place wasn't going to be so bad, after all.

I think some hearing people around us were learning something, too—even those three kids, who were still following us around.

Maybe they never thought about it before, but being deaf doesn't mean you can't hear or talk. You can hear with your eyes and talk with your hands.

◆ LIBRARY LINK ◆

If you enjoyed reading this story, you might enjoy reading The Seeing Stick *by Jane Yolen.*

 Reader's **Response**

Who might have had the hardest time getting used to the new town—Michael or his parents? Tell why.

SELECTION FOLLOW-UP

Words In Our Hands

 Questions

1. What were the different ways in which Michael's parents talked?
2. How did Michael's parents "hear" with their eyes?
3. Why did people in the new town stare at the family?
4. How did seeing *The Wooden Boy* make Michael feel? How do you know?
5. Why did Michael feel better about his family after seeing *The Wooden Boy*?

 Writing to Learn

THINK AND DECIDE   Do people "listen" with their eyes when they "talk" with their hands? Practice listening with your eyes. Tell what the children are saying with their gestures.

WRITE   What did you learn about deafness? Tell one thing you will remember if you speak with a person who is hearing impaired.

Words and Other Codes

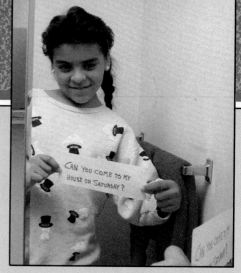

▲ This person is reading a mirror-code message.

You want to tell your friend a secret. No one else must know what you're saying. So the way to do it is to use a code that only the two of you will understand.

MEE TME AFT ERS CHO OL

See if you can figure out this secret message. It is a simple "space code." Words are broken up by spacing after every third letter. Here is what the code means:

MEET ME AFTER SCHOOL

Now try to figure this one out. You can figure it out by holding it up to a mirror!

CAN YOU COME TO MY HOUSE ON SATURDAY?

A sailor sends a message using semaphore flags. For the letter J, the flags are held in the three o'clock position.

J

276

A B C D E F G H I J K L M

Samuel Morse made it possible to send messages over long distances instantly with his invention, the telegraph. ▶

▲
In Morse Code, dots and dashes stand for letters and numbers.

Not all codes are written. For example, sailors use flags to send messages. They make letters of the alphabet by holding the flags in different positions. This kind of code is called semaphore.

In the 1830s, Samuel Morse invented a new way to send messages by wire. His code uses dots and dashes to make letters and numbers. Dot-dot-dot means "S." Dash-dash-dash means "O." Dot-dot-dot again means "S." *SOS* means that a ship is in trouble.

What do codes have to do with reading? When you were first starting to read, all words looked like a code to you. By now you have come a long way in breaking the reading code, a process that is sometimes called decoding. You will continue to read words that are new to you. If you think of them as codes to break, figuring out new words can be fun.

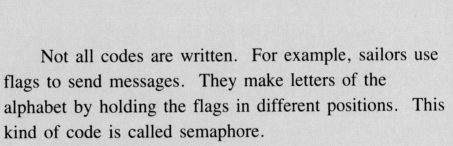

N O P Q R S T U V W X Y Z

In sports, messages to players often need to be kept secret from the other team. That's when sports signals become codes, and scratching an arm can mean something more than having an itch.

SPORTS SIGNALS

by Gary Apple

Imagine that you are the coach of a football team. Your team is behind by one point, and there is time for only one more play. The other team expects you to throw a long pass, but you decide to surprise them and run with the ball.

How do you communicate your plan to your players? You can't shout, "Surprise them by running instead of passing!" Your players may not hear you, and if they do, the other team will hear you, too. The surprise will be lost.

278

Can you tell which of these coaches is giving a signal?

Instead, you communicate by giving your team a secret signal using sign language. Before the game, you tell your team that if you put both hands on your head, it means to run with the ball. Your players read your signal and try to run with the ball. Success! Your team scores, and you win the game!

Sign language is used all the time in sports. Coaches signal players. Players signal other players. Officials signal players, and players signal officials. Everyone signals everybody!

Of course, signals aren't used only for secret plays. In football, for example, before a player catches a punt, he can wave his hand to signal a *fair catch*. With this signal the player makes a deal with the other team. It means, ''If you don't try to tackle me, I won't try to run with the ball when I catch it.''

Another sports signal that everyone understands and uses is the ''time-out'' sign. This is done by making a letter ''T'' with the hands. It tells the official to stop the clock. Football and basketball are two of the sports that use this sign.

Fair Catch!   **Time Out!**   **Safe!**

How many secret signals can you find in this picture?

Secret signals are used when one team doesn't want the other team to know what's going on. If you have ever watched a football game, you may have noticed a coach on the sidelines making strange movements. What he is doing is giving secret directions to the players on the field.

Football coaches can be very tricky. Sometimes, two coaches on the same team give signals at the same time. One coach gives the real secret play while the other gives signals that the players ignore. This is done to confuse the other team, so they don't know which signal is the real signal.

Baseball is the sport in which secret signals are used the most. When you watch a baseball game, it might look like the players are just waiting around for the next pitch. If you look closer, however, you will see that secret communications are being sent all over the field. If you see a player scratch his chin or a coach push his cap back on his head, there is a good chance that you have just seen a secret signal.

The catcher is about to signal for a certain type of pitch.

The pitcher and the catcher use sign language before every pitch. The catcher gives a sign to tell the pitcher the kind of pitch to throw. One finger may mean "Throw a fastball." Two fingers may mean "Pitch a curve ball." The catcher also uses a sign to tell the pitcher where to throw the pitch: inside, outside, high, or low. If the pitcher doesn't agree with the catcher, he will shake his head. The catcher will then secretly suggest another pitch.

Before every game, the catcher and the pitcher must talk about the sign language to be used. This way, there will be no mistakes. If a pitcher does not understand the signs, he might throw the wrong pitch, and the catcher may not be able to catch the ball.

The pitcher isn't the only one watching the catcher's secret signs. The second baseman and the shortstop also follow the sign language. If they know the kind of pitch to expect, they can guess where the ball will go if the batter hits it. The shortstop and second baseman have a set of secret signs of their own. They use them to tell the outfielders, who are far away and can't see the catcher, what kind of pitch is on the way. When a shortstop puts his hands on his knees, he might be telling the outfielders to expect a fastball.

The team that is up to bat also uses secret sign language. During a ballgame, coaches stand near first base and third base. Part of their job is to give secret directions to the batter. They also direct the runners who have reached a base. These coaches may seem to be just standing around, but don't be fooled. When they dust off their sleeve or hold their elbow, they may be telling the batter to bunt or the base runner to steal a base.

A base coach secretly signals batters and base runners.

283

Teams are always trying to find out what the other team's signals are. To stop this from happening, teams often change their signals during a game. A sign that meant ''steal the base'' in one inning may mean ''stay on base'' in another. Coaches can get even trickier than that. For example, base runners might be told to ignore all signs unless the coach's feet are in a certain position.

The next time you're at the ballpark or stadium, pay attention to the movements of the team members. See if you can tell which are secret signals and which are everyday movements. Players and coaches can be tricky, so watch carefully; but don't be too suspicious. When a coach scratches his chin, he might just have an itch!

◆ LIBRARY LINK ◆

If you would like to learn more about signals, you might enjoy reading Train Whistles *by Helen Roney Settler.*

Reader's Response

Do you think understanding sports signals will help you enjoy sports more? Why or why not?

SELECTION FOLLOW-UP

SPORTS SIGNALS

Questions

1. Why are signals used in sports?
2. How are the signals for *fair catch* and *time out* different from the other signals described?
3. Who gives secret signals in baseball?
4. A team often changes its secret signals. Why is this helpful? How might it be a problem? How did you decide on your answers?
5. In which sports do you think secret signals would not be useful?

Writing to Learn

THINK AND CREATE   You, also, may create a secret language. If you want to send a message in code, put the first letter of each word at the end. Read the code chart below.

Real Word	Code Word
sports	portss
signal	ignals
message	essagem

WRITE   Write a message to a friend. Write it in code. See if your friend can figure out the message.

285

READING NON-FICTION

Comprehension:

Making Comparisons

In "Sports Signals," you read about the special ways in which players and coaches communicate. The selection compared the signals used in various sports.

When you *compare* two or more things, you tell how they are alike and how they are different.

When writers compare, they often use word clues to help the reader. *Same*, *both*, and *too* mean the things being compared are alike. *However, but*, and *unlike* mean they are different.

Read this passage based on "Words in Our Hands." Use word clues to help you understand the comparison.

> Finger spelling and sign language are both ways to talk with your hands. Unlike sign language, finger spelling is easy to learn. Once you have learned sign language, however, it is much faster than finger spelling.

> Sign language and finger spelling are alike in some ways and different in others. This chart compares the two ways of talking with your hands.

COMPARISON OF HAND TALKING

	uses hands	easy to learn	fast
Finger Spelling	yes	yes	no
Sign Language	yes	no	yes

The chart shows that both ways of talking use hands. The chart also shows that finger spelling is easier to learn than sign language, but slower to use.

Using What You Have Learned

Read the paragraph below. Then write how baseball and basketball are alike and how they are different. A chart may help you compare the two sports.

> Baseball and basketball are alike in some ways. In both sports, the players use hand signals. Baseball players use signals that are secret. A basketball game moves so fast that secret signals would be hard for players to see. Most basketball signals are made openly.

As You Read

In "The Horse Who Lived Upstairs," notice how the main character compares his life with the life he thinks he wants.

The Horse Who Lived Upstairs

by Phyllis McGinley

Joey was a city horse who wanted to live in the country. Then one day, Joey got his wish!

There was once a horse named Joey who was discontented. He was discontented because he didn't live in a red barn with a weathervane on top like this, and he didn't live in a green meadow where he could run about and kick up his heels like this. Instead, he lived upstairs in a big brick building in New York.

Joey worked for Mr. Polaski, who sold fruits and vegetables to city people. Joey pulled the vegetable wagon through the city streets. And in New York, there isn't room for barns or meadows.

So every night when Joey came home, he stepped out from the shafts of the wagon and into an elevator, and up he went to his stall on the fourth floor of the big brick building. It was a fine stall and Joey was very comfortable there. He had plenty of oats to eat and plenty of fresh straw to lie on. He even had a window to look out of. But still Joey was discontented.

"How I long to sip fresh water from a babbling brook!" he often exclaimed. And then he would sniff discontentedly at the old bathtub near the elevator that served him as a watering trough.

It wasn't that he had to work hard. Mr. Polaski was kind to him and brought him home at five o'clock every day.

In the winter Joey had a blanket to wear on his back to keep him warm. And in the summertime Mr. Polaski got him a hat to wear on his head to keep him cool. And every day he had many interesting adventures. Sometimes he met a policeman who gave him sugar. Sometimes ladies patted him on the nose and fed him carrots. He was introduced to the high-bred horses who drew the hansom cabs along the plaza. He saw the children playing in the playgrounds and the parks. But it made no difference to Joey.

"This is no life for a horse," he used to say to the Percheron who lived in the next stall to him. "We city horses don't know what real living is. I want to move to the country and sleep in a red barn with a weathervane on top and kick up my heels in a green meadow."

So how happy he was when one day Mr. Polaski said to him, "Joey, I think I could sell more vegetables if I drove a truck. I will miss you, Joey, but you will like it on the farm where I am going to send you."

When Joey reached the country, sure enough, there was the barn with its weathervane, and there was the meadow.

"This is the life!" cried Joey to himself. But poor Joey! The barn was cold in winter and hot in summer. He didn't have a blanket and he didn't have a hat. And he had very little time to kick up his heels in the green meadow, for all day long he pulled a plow through the earth. A plow is harder to pull than a wagon, and besides, the farmer worked from sunrise to sundown instead of the eight hours Joey was used to. Sometimes they forgot to put fresh straw in his stall, and nobody thought to give him sugar or carrots. There were plenty of children but they climbed on his back and teased him when he wanted to eat. And instead of the Percheron, there was a cross old gray horse next to him, who looked down his nose at Joey because Joey knew so little about farm life.

One day, when he wasn't pulling a plow because it was Sunday, Joey saw several people picnicking in the meadow. He decided to join them, for they looked as if they came from the city, and he thought they might have a lump of sugar in one of their pockets.

When he reached the spot, they had gone for a walk, so he ate up their lunch. When they came back, they were very angry and Joey was shut up in his stall for the rest of the day. He didn't even have a window to look out of. He was lonely for his friends, the policeman and the ladies who patted him on the nose. He was lonely for the high-bred horses and all the interesting sights of the city.

"I don't think I belong in the country after all," sighed Joey. "I am now more discontented than ever."

Next day he heard the honk of a horn. He looked from the door of the barn, and whom should he see but Mr. Polaski, getting out of the truck!

"I have come for Joey," Mr. Polaski told the farmer. "I cannot get any more tires for my truck, so I think I will sell fruit and vegetables from my wagon again."

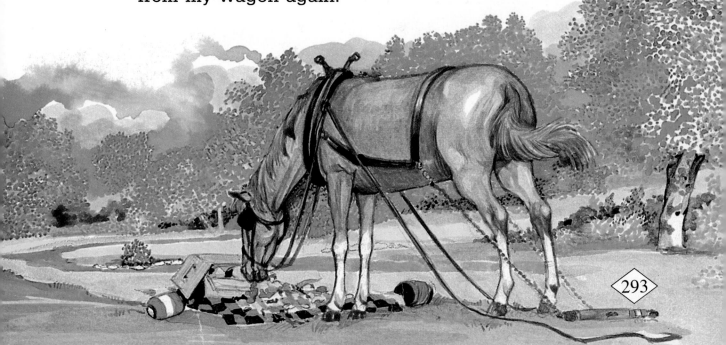

My goodness, but Joey was happy! He went back to the city with Mr. Polaski and got into the elevator, and up he went to the fourth floor of the big brick building. There was his stall, and there was the window for him to look out of. And there was the friendly Percheron.

"Welcome back, Joey," exclaimed the Percheron. "I have missed you. The policeman has missed you. The lady customers have missed you, and so have the children in the playgrounds and the parks. Tell me, how did you like the country?"

"The country is all right for country animals," Joey said, "but I guess I am just a city horse at heart."

And he was never discontented again.

 Reader's Response

Would you suggest this story to one of your friends? Why or why not?

The Horse Who Lived
Upstairs

Questions

1. What did Joey wish for?
2. How did people show that they cared about Joey? Tell how you got your answer.
3. Compare Joey's life in the city with his life on the farm.
4. What made Joey finally realize that he belonged in the city?
5. Do you think Mr. Polaski took Joey back because he really couldn't get tires for his truck? Explain.

Writing to Learn

THINK AND ANALYZE   How did Joey feel about the country before he went there? How did he feel about it after he got there? Copy and finish the chart below.

How Joey Felt About the Country...		
	Before He Went There	After He Went There
	The country was nice.	

WRITE   Read what you wrote in the chart. Then write a sentence to tell how you think Joey might have felt when Mr. Polaski said, "I have come for Joey."

A young woman expresses kindness to everyone she meets. Even the king learns of her goodness— in a most surprising way.

MUFARO'S
Beautiful
DAUGHTERS
AN AFRICAN TALE

written and illustrated by John Steptoe

A long time ago, in a certain place in Africa,
a small village lay across a river and half a day's
journey from a city where a great king lived. A man
named Mufaro (əm fä′ rō) lived in this village with his
two daughters, who were called Manyara (män yä′ rə)
and Nyasha (nyä′ shə). Everyone agreed that Manyara
and Nyasha were very beautiful.

297

Manyara was almost always in a bad temper. She teased her sister whenever their father's back was turned, and she had been heard to say, "Someday, Nyasha, I will be a queen, and you will be a servant in my household."

"If that should come to pass," Nyasha responded, "I will be pleased to serve you. But why do you say such things? You are clever and strong and beautiful. Why are you so unhappy?"

"Because everyone talks about how kind *you* are, and they praise everything you do," Manyara replied. "I'm certain that Father loves you best. But when I am a queen, everyone will know that your silly kindness is only weakness."

Nyasha was sad that Manyara felt this way, but she ignored her sister's words and went about her chores. Nyasha kept a small plot of land, on which she grew millet, sunflowers, yams, and vegetables. She always sang as she worked, and some said it was her singing that made her crops more bountiful than anyone else's.

One day, Nyasha noticed a small garden snake resting beneath a yam vine. "Good day, little Nyoka (nyō' kä)," she called to him. "You are welcome here. You will keep away any creatures who might spoil my vegetables." She bent forward, gave the little snake a loving pat on the head, and then returned to her work.

From that day on, Nyoka was always at Nyasha's side when she tended her garden. It was said that she sang all the more sweetly when he was there.

Mufaro knew nothing of how Manyara treated Nyasha. Nyasha was too considerate of her father's feelings to complain, and Manyara was always careful to behave herself when Mufaro was around.

Early one morning, a messenger from the city arrived. The Great King wanted a wife. "The Most Worthy and Beautiful Daughters in the Land are invited to appear before the King, and he will choose one to become Queen!" the messenger proclaimed.

Mufaro called Manyara and Nyasha to him. "It would be a great honor to have one of you chosen," he said. "Prepare yourselves to journey to the city. I will call together all our friends to make a wedding party. We will leave tomorrow as the sun rises."

"But, my father," Manyara said sweetly, "it would be painful for either of us to leave you, even to be wife to the king. I know Nyasha would grieve to death if she were parted from you. I am strong. Send me to the city, and let poor Nyasha be happy here with you."

Mufaro beamed with pride. "The king has asked for the most worthy and the most beautiful. No, Manyara, I cannot send you alone. Only a king can choose between two such worthy daughters. Both of you must go!"

That night, when everyone was asleep, Manyara stole quietly out of the village. She had never been in the forest at night before, and she was frightened, but her greed to be the first to appear before the king drove her on. In her hurry, she almost stumbled over a small boy who suddenly appeared, standing in the path.

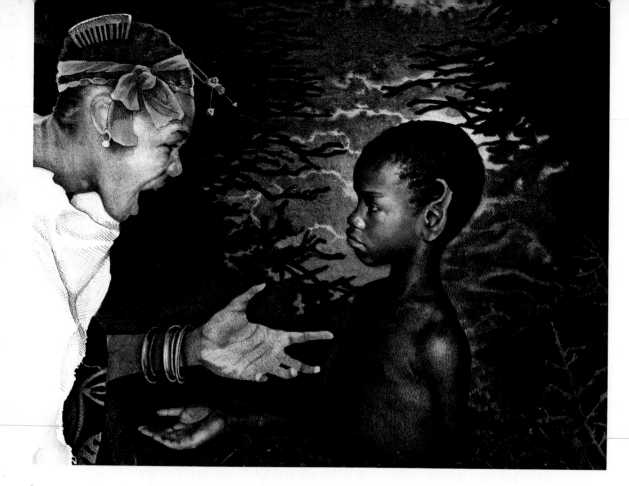

"Please," said the boy. "I am hungry. Will you give me something to eat?"

"I have brought only enough for myself," Manyara replied.

"But, please!" said the boy. "I am so *very* hungry."

"Out of my way, boy! Tomorrow I will become your queen. How dare you stand in my path?"

After traveling for what seemed to be a great distance, Manyara came to a small clearing. There, silhouetted against the moonlight, was an old woman seated on a large stone.

The old woman spoke. "I will give you some advice, Manyara. Soon after you pass the place where two paths cross, you will see a grove of trees. They will laugh at you. You must not laugh in return. Later, you will meet a man with his head under his arm. You must be polite to him."

"How do you know my name? How dare you advise your future queen? Stand aside, you ugly old woman!" Manyara scolded, and then rushed on her way without looking back.

Just as the old woman had foretold, Manyara came to a grove of trees, and they did indeed seem to be laughing at her.

"I must be calm," Manyara thought. "I will *not* be frightened." She looked up at the trees and laughed out loud. "I laugh at you, trees!" she shouted, and she hurried on.

It was not yet dawn when Manyara heard the sound of rushing water. "The river must be up ahead," she thought. "The great city is just on the other side."

But there, on the rise, she saw a man with his head tucked under his arm. Manyara ran past him without speaking. "A queen acknowledges only those who please her," she said to herself. "I will be queen. I will be queen," she chanted, as she hurried on toward the city.

Nyasha woke at the first light of dawn. As she put on her finest garments, she thought how her life might be changed forever beyond this day. "I'd much prefer to live here," she admitted to herself. "I'd hate to leave this village and never see my father or sing to little Nyoka again."

Her thoughts were interrupted by loud shouts and a commotion from the wedding party assembled outside. Manyara was missing! Everyone bustled about, searching and calling for her. When they found her footprints on the path that led to the city, they decided to go on as planned.

As the wedding party moved through the forest, brightly plumed birds darted about in the cool green shadows beneath the trees. Though anxious about her sister, Nyasha was soon filled with excitement about all there was to see.

They were deep in the forest when she saw the small boy standing by the side of the path.

"You must be hungry," she said, and handed him a yam she had brought for her lunch. The boy smiled and disappeared as quietly as he had come.

Later, as they were approaching the place where the two paths crossed, the old woman appeared and silently pointed the way to the city. Nyasha thanked her and gave her a small pouch filled with sunflower seeds.

The sun was high in the sky when the party
came to the grove of towering trees. Their uppermost
branches seemed to bow down to Nyasha as she
passed beneath them.

At last, someone announced that they were near
their destination.

Nyasha ran ahead and topped the rise before the
others could catch up with her. She stood transfixed
at her first sight of the city. "Oh, my father," she
called. "A great spirit must stand guard here! Just
look at what lies before us. I never in all my life
dreamed there could be anything so beautiful!"

Arm in arm, Nyasha and her father descended the
hill, crossed the river, and approached the city gate.
Just as they entered through the great doors, the air
was rent by piercing cries, and Manyara ran wildly
out of a chamber at the center of the enclosure.
When she saw Nyasha, she fell upon her, sobbing.

"Do not go to the king, my sister. Oh, please, Father, do not let her go!" she cried hysterically. "There's a great monster there, a snake with five heads! He said that he knew all my faults and that I displeased him. He would have swallowed me alive if I had not run. Oh, my sister, please do not go inside that place."

It frightened Nyasha to see her sister so upset. But, leaving her father to comfort Manyara, she bravely made her way to the chamber and opened the door.

On the seat of the great chief's stool lay the little garden snake. Nyasha laughed with relief and joy.

"My little friend," she exclaimed. "It's such a pleasure to see you, but why are you here?"

"I am the king," Nyoka replied.

And there, before Nyasha's eyes, the garden snake changed shape.

"I am the king. I am also the hungry boy with whom you shared a yam in the forest and the old woman to whom you made a gift of sunflower seeds. But you know me best as Nyoka. Because I have been all of these, I know you to be the Most Worthy and Most Beautiful Daughter in the Land. It would make me very happy if you would be my wife."

307

And so it was that, a long time ago, Nyasha agreed to be married. The king's mother and sisters took Nyasha to their house, and the wedding preparations began. The best weavers in the land laid out their finest cloth for her wedding garments. Villagers from all around were invited to the celebration, and a great feast was held. Nyasha prepared the bread for the wedding feast from millet that had been brought from her village.

Mufaro declared to all who would hear him that he was the happiest father in all the land, for he was blessed with two beautiful and worthy daughters— Nyasha, the queen; and Manyara, a servant in the queen's household.

◆ LIBRARY LINK ◆

If you enjoyed reading this story by John Steptoe, you might like to read other books by this author, such as Train Ride.

Reader's Response

What pictures does this story create in your mind?

MUFARO'S BEAUTIFUL DAUGHTERS

 ## Questions

1. How did Manyara feel toward her sister?
2. What was the real reason Manyara told her father that Nyasha should not leave home?
3. Why did the king appear to the sisters in so many different forms?
4. How did the king test Manyara and Nyasha? Tell some of the ways.
5. Do you think Manyara's behavior changed after what happened to her? How did you reach this conclusion?

 ## Writing to Learn

THINK AND INVENT Many characters are in this story: Mufaro, Manyara, Nyasha, and the king who takes many shapes and forms. Read the character riddle below.

Character Riddle

I am a little creature.
I stay by Nyasha's side.
I like to hear her sing.
Who am I?

(Nyoka the snake)

WRITE Write a character riddle about one of the characters in the story. You may tell what the character says or does. See if others can guess your riddle.

Vocabulary:

Multiple Meanings

Have you noticed that many words have more than one meaning? When you read a new word, become a detective! Be alert and look for clues to its correct meaning. A good detective checks as many clues as possible.

First, look at the other words in the sentence that may give you clues about the word. For example, in the story "Mufaro's Beautiful Daughters," you read the following:

> Nyasha kept a small plot of land, on which she grew millet, sunflowers, yams, and vegetables.

The word *plot* has more than one meaning. *Plot* means "a secret plan," "all the happenings in the main story of a novel, play, and so on," and "a piece of ground." What does *plot* mean in the sentence above? Use context clues to figure out its meaning. The words *land* and *grew* help you know that plot means "a piece of ground."

Now read the following:

> That night, when everyone was asleep, Manyara stole quietly out of the village.

Does the word *stole* mean "ran to the next base safely," "moved in a quiet way," or "robbed"? How can you tell? What context clues helped you?

Next, look for clues in your dictionary. This is how the dictionary explains the word *dawn,* for example.

dawn (dôn) **v.** **1** to begin to grow light as the sun rises [Day is *dawning*.] **2** to come into being; begin to develop [With the discovery of electricity, a new age *dawned*.] **3** to begin to be understood or felt [The meaning suddenly *dawned* on me.] ◆**n.** **1** the beginning of day; daybreak. **2** the beginning of anything [the *dawn* of the Space Age].

Read the following sentences.

Since it will be a long trip, we'll leave at *dawn*.
Computers brought about the *dawn* of a new age.

Which dictionary meaning describes the way the word is used in each sentence?

Using What You Have Learned

1. What does the word *past* mean in the following sentence? What context clues helped you with its meaning?

Manyara ran *past* him without speaking.

2. Can you think of two meanings for the word *bark?*
3. Write two sentences using two different meanings of the word *watch*.

As You Read

As you read "The Boy Who Cried Wolf," use context clues to help you figure out words with more than one meaning.

In this play, a young shepherd boy learns a lesson . . . and so do we.

The Boy Who Cried
WOLF

from the fable by Aesop
adapted by Genie Iverson

Characters: Storyteller   Little Girl
Shepherd Boy   First Farmhand
Father   Second Farmhand
Old Woman   Third Farmhand
Farmer

ACT ONE

Storyteller: A shepherd boy and his father stand talking on a hillside. Their sheep move about them.

Father: Are you ready to look after these sheep by yourself, son? It's time for me to go back to the village.

Shepherd Boy: (*uncertain*) I think so, Papa.

Father: I'll help you herd our sheep here each morning. And I'll come back at sunset to help you drive them home. But you must stay with them during the day.

Shepherd Boy: Yes, Papa. Only . . . (*looking around*) . . . I don't think I'll like being up here alone.

Father: Alone? Nonsense! Look down there at the road. People come and go all day.

Shepherd Boy: But they never stop.

Father: Maybe they don't stop. But they will come if you ever need help. Just call. (*handing boy the crook*) I have to go now. But I'll be back at sunset. (Father *leaves and the shepherd sits down to watch his sheep.*)

Storyteller: Slowly—very slowly the morning passes. The young shepherd boy feels more and more alone.

Shepherd Boy: I don't like staying here all day by myself. (*sighs*) It's lonely here.

Storyteller: Looking down the hill, the shepherd boy sees an old woman walking along the road. Pails of milk swing from a pole across her shoulders.

Shepherd Boy: I wish that old woman would stop and visit. I wish . . . (*pause*) . . . I know what I'll do! (*leaps up waving his crook*) Help! Help! A WOLF is after my sheep!

Storyteller: The old woman hurries up the hill to help. Milk splashes from her pails.

Old Woman: (*winded*) Where? . . . Where is the wolf? We can chase him with my pole!

Shepherd Boy: (*looking down*) There is no wolf. I wanted you to stop and visit. So I played a trick on you.

Old Woman: No wolf! You mean you made me run up this hill for nothing? What is the matter with you, boy?

Shepherd Boy: I didn't mean any harm.

Old Woman: (*picking up her pails*) Hummf! Just look at these pails! Empty! All that good milk . . . spilled for nothing.

Shepherd Boy: I just wanted you to stop and visit. . . .

Old Woman: Tricking folks is a sorry business. I came to visit you today, but trouble may be your visitor tomorrow. Mark my words. (*walking away muttering*) He'll be sorry . . . sorry indeed. Just wait and see!

ACT TWO

Storyteller: It is the next morning. The unhappy shepherd boy sits on the hillside. As his sheep move about him, he thinks about the long, lonely day ahead.

Shepherd Boy: (*wearily*) Nibble . . . Nibble . . . Nibble!
Baaaa! . . . Baaaa! . . . Baaaa!
Nibble . . . Baaaa!
Baaaa! . . . Nibble! (*long sigh*)
All day long . . . that's all you old sheep ever do!

Storyteller: The shepherd boy hears the rumble of a cart.

Shepherd Boy: Listen! Someone's coming! (*stands and looks down the hill*)

Storyteller: A farmer and his little girl appear on the road, pulling a cart filled with turnips.

Shepherd Boy: Do I dare call out again that there is a wolf? If I do . . . maybe they'll stop. . . . (*pause*) . . . Help! Help! A wolf is after my sheep!

Storyteller: The farmer leaves his cart and runs up the hill to help. His little girl hurries along behind.

Farmer: Where? Where's the wolf?

Little Girl: (*afraid*) Is the wolf hiding behind that tree? Will he eat me?

Farmer: I don't see any wolf. (*looking around*) There's no wolf here!

Shepherd Boy: It was just a trick.

Farmer: (*angrily*) You called for help when you didn't need it! Shame on you!

Shepherd Boy: Please don't be angry. I get lonely sitting here all day by myself.

Farmer: (*taking* little girl *by hand*) Come along, child. This boy has wasted enough of our time with his tricks. But someday he'll be sorry.

Little Girl: (*as they walk away*) Why will he be sorry, Papa?

Farmer: Because tricks bring trouble. Just wait and see. What that boy did today will be remembered tomorrow. (*They exit.*)

ACT THREE
(Scene One)

Storyteller: It is another bright, cool morning. The shepherd boy has watched his flock since sunrise. He is bored and lonely.

Shepherd Boy: Same old hillside! (*sigh*) Same old sheep! Same old grass! And the sun is not even overhead yet. It's still morning! (*long sigh*) Maybe I'll sit and watch the road. Somebody should be coming along soon.

Storyteller: The shepherd boy is about to sit when he hears a loud growl. He turns. A wolf is crouched near his flock.

Shepherd Boy: A WOLF! (*He crawls behind a rock and peeks out.*) A REAL wolf! What can I do!

Storyteller: As the wolf creeps nearer to the frightened sheep, singing is heard from the road below.

Farmhands: (*offstage*) Hey, ho! Hey, ho!
It's to the fields we go,
With hoe and rake,
With rake and hoe,
Hey, ho! Hey, ho!

Storyteller: Three farmhands come into view. The shepherd boy runs to the top of the hill shouting.

Shepherd Boy: (*waving his crook*) HELP! HELP! A WOLF is after my sheep!

First Farmhand: (*stopping*) Look. It's that shepherd boy! The one folks are talking about.

Second Farmhand: They say he cries "wolf" when there is no wolf.

Third Farmhand: (*nodding*) Foolish boy! You can't believe a word he says.

Shepherd Boy: (*calling as loudly as he can*) Hurry! Hurry! The wolf is taking my sheep!

First Farmhand: (*calling to shepherd*) We DON'T believe you!

Second Farmhand: That's right! We've heard about you and your tricks.

Third Farmhand: You can't fool us! We know there is no wolf! (*The farmhands walk away laughing.*)

Shepherd Boy: Come back! Come back! This ISN'T a trick. This time there IS a wolf! A REAL wolf! . . . (*sobs*) . . . He is running away with my sheep. (*The boy sits down, covers his face with his hands and cries.*)

(Scene Two)

Storyteller: It is sunset. The shepherd sits with his head in his hands. The wolf is gone. But so are some of the sheep. Father approaches.

Father: Are you ready to take the sheep home?

Shepherd Boy: Oh yes, Papa! But some of the sheep are gone! A wolf came—a great big wolf!

Father: A wolf! Did you call for help?

Shepherd Boy: Yes, Papa. Yes. There were men on the road. I called. But they wouldn't come. (*lowering his eyes*) They thought that I was playing a trick.

Father: (*puzzled*) A trick?

Shepherd Boy: (*hanging his head*) Before when I was lonely, I cried "wolf" so that people would stop and visit. Then . . . then there really was a wolf. And I called. But they didn't believe me.

Father: (*sitting down on a rock*) Well . . . have you learned something?

Shepherd Boy: (*sitting down beside his father*) Yes, Papa. I learned that I should always tell the truth . . . (*pause*) . . . because if I don't, people won't believe me when I do.

THE END

◆ LIBRARY LINK ◆

If you enjoyed this play based on a tale by Aesop, you might want to read Aesop's Fables, *edited by Anne White, or* Tales from Aesop, *edited by Harold Jones.*

 Reader's Response

How did you feel about the lesson in this play?

322

The Boy Who Cried WOLF

 ## Questions

1. Why did the boy call for help the first two times?
2. What did the farmer mean when he said that what the boy did today would be remembered tomorrow?
3. Was the farmer correct? Tell why or why not.
4. Why do you think that the boy's father didn't punish him?
5. What words would you use to describe the boy in this story? Why did you choose these words?

 ## Writing to Learn

THINK AND IMAGINE The young shepherd boy learns many things about himself and his friends. Imagine what he might have written in his journal.

> One day, a real wolf
> came and

WRITE Pretend you are the shepherd boy. On a page of your notebook, write about your frightening day. Tell how your adventure may have changed your life forever.

Sometimes, as friends talk, the message gets all mixed up. This certainly is true for Piglet and Pooh.

In Which Piglet Meets a Heffalump

from
Winnie-the-Pooh

written by A. A. Milne
illustrated by Ernest H. Shepard

Piglet and Winnie-the-Pooh are two of Christopher Robin's stuffed animals. He brings them to life in his imagination, where they have many interesting and funny adventures.

One day, when Christopher Robin and Winnie-the-Pooh and Piglet were all talking together, Christopher Robin finished the mouthful he was eating and said carelessly: "I saw a Heffalump to-day, Piglet."

"What was it doing?" asked Piglet.

"Just lumping along," said Christopher Robin. "I don't think it saw *me*."

"I saw one once," said Piglet. "At least, I think I did," he said. "Only perhaps it wasn't."

"So did I," said Pooh, wondering what a Heffalump was like.

"You don't often see them," said Christopher Robin carelessly.

"Not now," said Piglet.

"Not at this time of year," said Pooh.

Then they all talked about something else, until it was time for Pooh and Piglet to go home together.

At first as they stumped along the path which edged the Hundred Acre Wood, they didn't say much to each other; but when they came to the stream and had helped each other across the stepping stones, and were able to walk side by side again over the heather, they began to talk in a friendly way about this and that, and Piglet said, "If you see what I mean, Pooh," and Pooh said, "It's just what I think myself, Piglet," and Piglet said, "But, on the other hand, Pooh, we must remember," and Pooh said, "Quite true, Piglet, although I had forgotten it for the moment." And then, just as they came to the Six Pine Trees, Pooh looked round to see that nobody else was listening, and said in a very solemn voice:

"Piglet, I have decided something."

"What have you decided, Pooh?"

"I have decided to catch a Heffalump."

Pooh nodded his head several times as he said this, and waited for Piglet to say "How?" or "Pooh, you couldn't!" or something helpful of that sort, but Piglet said nothing. The fact was Piglet was wishing that *he* had thought about it first.

"I shall do it," said Pooh, after waiting a little longer, "by means of a trap. And it must be a Cunning Trap, so you will have to help me, Piglet."

"Pooh," said Piglet, feeling quite happy again now, "I will." And then he said, "How shall we do it?" and Pooh said, "That's just it. How?" And then they sat down together to think it out.

Pooh's first idea was that they should dig a Very Deep Pit, and then the Heffalump would come along and fall into the Pit, and——

"Why?" said Piglet.

"Why what?" said Pooh.

"Why would he fall in?"

Pooh rubbed his nose with his paw, and said that the Heffalump might be walking along, humming a little song, and looking up at the sky, wondering if it would rain, and so he wouldn't see the Very Deep Pit until he was half-way down, when it would be too late.

Piglet said that this was a very good Trap, but supposing it were raining already?

Pooh rubbed his nose again, and said that he hadn't thought of that. And then he brightened up, and said that, if it were raining already, the Heffalump

 would be looking at the sky wondering if it would *clear up,* and so he wouldn't see the Very Deep Pit until he was half-way down. . . . When it would be too late.

Piglet said that, now that this point had been explained, he thought it was a Cunning Trap.

Pooh was very proud when he heard this, and he felt that the Heffalump was as good as caught already, but there was just one other thing which had to be thought about, and it was this. *Where should they dig the Very Deep Pit?*

Piglet said that the best place would be somewhere where a Heffalump was, just before he fell into it, only about a foot farther on.

"But then he would see us digging it," said Pooh.

"Not if he was looking at the sky."

"He would Suspect," said Pooh, "if he happened to look down." He thought for a long time and then added sadly, "It isn't as easy as I thought. I suppose that's why Heffalumps hardly *ever* get caught."

"That must be it," said Piglet.

They sighed and got up; and when they had taken a few gorse prickles out of themselves they sat down again; and all the time Pooh was saying to himself, "If only I could *think* of something!" For he felt sure that a Very Clever Brain could catch a Heffalump if only he knew the right way to go about it.

"Suppose," he said to Piglet, "*you* wanted to catch *me*, how would you do it?"

"Well," said Piglet, "I should do it like this. I should make a Trap, and I should put a Jar of Honey in the Trap, and you would smell it, and you would go in after it, and——"

"And I would go in after it," said Pooh excitedly, "only very carefully so as not to hurt myself, and I would get to the Jar of Honey, and I should lick round the edges first of all, pretending that there wasn't any more, you know, and then I should walk away and think about it a little, and then I should come back and start licking in the middle of the jar, and then——"

"Yes, well never mind about that. There you would be, and there I should catch you. Now the first thing to think of is, What do Heffalumps like? I should think acorns, shouldn't you? We'll get a lot of—I say, wake up, Pooh!"

Pooh, who had gone into a happy dream, woke up with a start, and said that Honey was a much more trappy thing than Haycorns. Piglet didn't think so; and they were just going to argue about it, when Piglet remembered that, if they put acorns in the Trap, *he* would have to find the acorns, but if they put honey, then Pooh would have to give up some of his own honey, so he said, "All right, honey then," just as Pooh remembered it too, and was going to say, "All right, haycorns."

"Honey," said Piglet to himself in a thoughtful way, as if it were now settled. "*I'll* dig the pit, while *you* go and get the honey."

"Very well," said Pooh, and he stumped off.

As soon as he got home, he went to the larder; and he stood on a chair, and took down a very large jar of honey from the top shelf.

It had HUNNY written on it, but, just to make sure, he took off the paper cover and looked at it, and it *looked* just like honey. "But you never can tell," said Pooh. "I remember my uncle saying once that he had seen cheese just this colour." So he put his tongue in, and took a large lick. "Yes," he said, "it is. No doubt about that. And honey, I should say, right down to the bottom of the jar. Unless, of course," he said, "somebody put cheese in the bottom just for a joke. Perhaps I had better go a *little* further . . . just in case . . . in case Heffalumps *don't* like cheese . . . same as me. . . . Ah!" And he gave a deep sigh. "I *was* right. It *is* honey, right the way down."

Having made certain of this, he took the jar back to Piglet, and Piglet looked up from the bottom of his Very Deep Pit, and said, "Got it?" and Pooh said, "Yes, but it isn't quite a full jar," and he threw it down to Piglet, and Piglet said, "No, it isn't! Is that all you've got left?" and Pooh said "Yes." Because it was. So Piglet put the jar at the bottom of the Pit, and climbed out, and they went off home together.

"Well, good night, Pooh," said Piglet, when they had got to Pooh's house. "And we meet at six o'clock tomorrow morning by the Pine Trees, and see how many Heffalumps we've got in our Trap."

"Six o'clock, Piglet. And have you got any string?"

"No. Why do you want string?"

"To lead them home with."

"Oh! . . . I *think* Heffalumps come if you whistle."

"Some do and some don't. You never can tell with Heffalumps. Well, good night!"

"Good night!"

And off Piglet trotted to his house TRESPASSERS W, while Pooh made his preparations for bed.

Some hours later, just as the night was beginning to steal away, Pooh woke up suddenly with a sinking feeling. He had had that sinking feeling before, and he knew what it meant. *He was hungry.* So he went to the larder, and he stood on a chair and reached up to the top shelf, and found—nothing.

"That's funny," he thought. "I know I had a jar of honey there. A full jar, full of honey right up to the top, and it had HUNNY written on it, so that I should know it was honey. That's very funny." And then he began to wander up and down, wondering where it was and murmuring a murmur to himself. Like this:

It's very, very funny,
'Cos I *know* I had some honey;
'Cos it had a label on,
    Saying HUNNY.

A goloptious full-up pot too,
And I don't know where it's got to,
No, I don't know where it's gone—
    Well, it's funny.

He had murmured this to himself three times in a singing sort of way, when suddenly he remembered. He had put it into the Cunning Trap to catch the Heffalump.

"Bother!" said Pooh. "It all comes of trying to be kind to Heffalumps." And he got back into bed.

But he couldn't sleep. The more he tried to sleep, the more he couldn't. He tried Counting Sheep, which is sometimes a good way of getting to sleep, and, as that was no good, he tried counting Heffalumps. And that was worse. Because every Heffalump that he counted was making straight for a pot of Pooh's honey, *and eating it all*. For some minutes he lay there miserably, but when the five hundred and eighty-seventh Heffalump was licking its jaws, and saying to itself, "Very good honey this, I don't know when I've tasted better," Pooh could bear it no longer. He jumped out of bed, he ran out of the house, and he ran straight to the Six Pine Trees.

The Sun was still in bed, but there was a lightness in the sky over the Hundred Acre Wood which seemed to show that it was waking up and would soon be kicking off the clothes. In the half-light the Pine Trees looked cold and lonely, and the Very Deep Pit seemed deeper than it was, and Pooh's jar of honey at the bottom was something mysterious, a shape and no more. But as he got nearer to it his nose told him that it was indeed honey, and his tongue came out and began to polish up his mouth, ready for it.

"Bother!" said Pooh, as he got his nose inside the jar. "A Heffalump has been eating it!" And then he thought a little and said, "Oh, no, *I* did. I forgot."

Indeed, he had eaten most of it. But there was a little left at the very bottom of the jar, and he pushed his head right in, and began to lick. . . .

By and by Piglet woke up. As soon as he woke he said to himself, "Oh!" Then he said bravely, "Yes," and then, still more bravely, "Quite so." But he didn't feel very brave, for the word which was really jiggeting about in his brain was "Heffalumps."

What was a Heffalump like?

Was it Fierce?

Did it come when you whistled? And *how* did it come?

Was it Fond of Pigs at all?

If it was Fond of Pigs, did it make any difference *what sort of Pig?*

Supposing it was Fierce with Pigs, would it make any difference *if the Pig had a grandfather called TRESPASSERS WILLIAM?*

He didn't know the answer to any of these questions . . . and he was going to see his first Heffalump in about an hour from now!

Of course Pooh would be with him, and it was much more Friendly with two. But suppose Heffalumps were Very Fierce with Pigs *and* Bears? Wouldn't it be better to pretend that he had a headache, and couldn't go up to the Six Pine Trees this morning? But then suppose that it was a very fine day, and there was no Heffalump in the trap, here he would be, in bed all the morning, simply wasting his time for nothing. What should he do?

And then he had a Clever Idea. He would go up very quietly to the Six Pine Trees now, peep very cautiously into the Trap, and see if there *was* a Heffalump there. And if there was, he would go back to bed, and if there wasn't, he wouldn't.

So off he went. At first he thought that there wouldn't be a Heffalump in the Trap, and then he thought that there would, and as he got nearer he was *sure* that there would, because he could hear it heffalumping about it like anything.

"Oh, dear, oh, dear, oh, dear!" said Piglet to himself. And he wanted to run away. But somehow, having got so near, he felt that he must just see what a Heffalump was like. So he crept to the side of the Trap and looked in. . . .

And all the time Winnie-the-Pooh had been trying to get the honey-jar off his head. The more he shook it, the more tightly it stuck. "*Bother!*" he said, inside the jar, and "*Oh, help!*" and, mostly "*Ow!*" And he tried bumping it against things, but as he couldn't see what he was bumping it against, it didn't help him, and he tried to climb out of the Trap, but as he could see nothing but jar, and not much of that, he couldn't find his way. So at last he lifted up his head, jar and all, and made a loud, roaring noise of Sadness and Despair . . . and it was at that moment that Piglet looked down.

"Help, help!" cried Piglet, "a Heffalump, a Horrible Heffalump!" and he scampered off as hard as he could, still crying out, "Help, help, a Herrible Hoffalump! Hoff, Hoff, a Hellible Horralump! Holl, Holl, a Hoffable Hellerump!" And he didn't stop crying and scampering until he got to Christopher Robin's house.

"Whatever's the matter, Piglet?" said Christopher Robin who was just getting up.

"Heff," said Piglet, breathing so hard that he could hardly speak, "a Hell—a Heff—a Heffalump."

"Where?"

"Up there," said Piglet, waving his paw.

"What did it look like?"

"Like—like——It had the biggest head you ever saw, Christopher Robin. A great enormous thing, like—like nothing. A huge big—well, like a—I don't know—like an enormous big nothing. Like a jar."

"Well," said Christopher Robin, putting on his shoes, "I shall go and look at it. Come on."

Piglet wasn't afraid if he had Christopher Robin with him, so off they went. . . .

"I can hear it, can't you?" said Piglet anxiously, as they got near.

"I can hear *something*," said Christopher Robin.

It was Pooh bumping his head against a tree-root he had found.

"There!" said Piglet. "Isn't it *awful?*" And he held on tight to Christopher Robin's hand.

Suddenly Christopher Robin began to laugh . . . and he laughed . . . and he laughed . . . and he laughed. And while he was still laughing—*Crash* went the Heffalump's head against the tree-root, Smash went the jar, and out came Pooh's head again. . . .

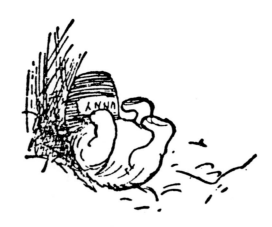

Then Piglet saw what a Foolish Piglet he had been, and he was so ashamed of himself that he ran straight off home and went to bed with a headache. But Christopher Robin and Pooh went home to breakfast together.

"Oh, Bear!" said Christopher Robin. "How I do love you!"

"So do I," said Pooh.

◆ LIBRARY LINK ◆

This story was taken from the book Winnie-the-Pooh. *You might enjoy reading the entire book to learn more about Pooh and his friends and all the fun they have together.*

 Reader's Response

If you could talk with Piglet and Pooh, what questions would you ask them?

WRITING ABOUT READING

Writing a Character Riddle

This unit was about characters who sent and received messages in different ways. A character riddle is a message that asks you to guess who the story character is. The clues are from the story, and you can use those clues to guess the character. The clues are written in the order in which they come in the story.

Here is a character riddle. See if you can figure out who the character is.

◆ I want to run about and kick up my heels.

◆ I want to sleep in a red barn.

◆ I want to sip water from a bubbling brook.

◆ Who am I?

Did you get the message? Did you guess the horse in ''The Horse Who Lived Upstairs''? Now you are going to write a character riddle, and your classmates are going to try to solve it.

Prewriting

Choose and draw a favorite character. Then draw five lines next to your character. On each line, write something the character does. This diagram will help you think of clues for your riddle.

Run about.

Want to live in a green meadow.

Kick up my heels.

Want to sip water from a bubbling brook.

Want to sleep in a real barn.

Writing

Choose three interesting details from your diagram. Use the details to write a riddle about the character. Write the clues as if *you* are the character. Put the clues in the same order as they are in the story. End your riddle with the question "Who am I?"

Revising

Read your character riddle to a partner. Can your partner guess which character the riddle is about? If not, add more details to your clues.

Proofreading

Use a dictionary to check your spelling. Be sure you began the first word of each sentence with a capital letter. Make a neat copy of your riddle.

Publishing

Make a character-riddle game with index cards. You and your classmates can try to guess the answers to each other's riddles.

WORKING TOGETHER

Sending a Message Without Words •••••••••••••••••••

In this unit you read how coaches send messages to their players without using words. Many people send messages without words. Have you ever seen a police officer directing traffic? Your group will practice sending a message without words.

Group members should do one or more of these tasks:

- ◆ Look at others when they talk.
- ◆ Record everyone's ideas on a list.
- ◆ Ask questions.
- ◆ Help group members understand what they should do.

Begin by talking about messages you might want to send. You might ask people to do something, go somewhere, or give you something, such as a pencil or a book. Take turns giving ideas for possible messages. Make a list of everyone's ideas. Together, choose one of them. Then discuss how a person could send the message without using words. Everyone should suggest ideas.

Try out the ideas on each other. If the message isn't easy to understand, think of ways to make it clearer. Then talk about when you might use this way of sending messages.

BOOKS TO ENJOY

Train Whistles by Helen Roney Sattler *(Lothrop, 1984)* The toots of a train whistle are a way for trains to signal to other trains, from one car of the train to another, and to people. Example: Two long toots, one short, and a long mean, ''Stop, cars and people! Wait until the train has passed!''

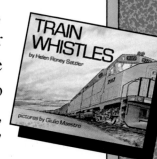

Computers by Jane Jonas Srivastava *(Harper & Row, 1972)* This book explains the basic units common to all computers and the kinds of tasks people program them to do.

The Seeing Stick by Jane Yolen *(Harper & Row, 1977)* This is the Chinese tale of an emperor who is sad because his daughter is blind. An old man says he can help her see with his ''seeing stick.''

Finger Rhymes by Marc Brown *(Dutton, 1980)* Fourteen familiar rhymes are presented.

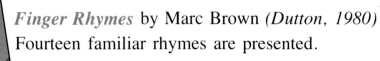

◆ GLOSSARY ◆

Full pronunciation key* The pronunciation of each word is shown just after the word, in this way: **abbreviate** (ə brē′vē āt).

The letters and signs used are pronounced as in the words below.

The mark ′ is placed after a syllable with a primary or heavy accent as in the example above.

The mark ′ after a syllable shows a secondary or lighter accent, as in **abbreviation** (ə brē′vē ā′shən).

SYMBOL	KEY WORDS	SYMBOL	KEY WORDS	SYMBOL	KEY WORDS
a	ask, fat	u	up, cut	r	red, dear
ā	ape, date	ur	fur, fern	s	sell, pass
ä	car, father			t	top, hat
		ə	a in ago	v	vat, have
e	elf, ten		e in agent	w	will, always
er	berry, care		e in father	y	yet, yard
ē	even, meet		i in unity	z	zebra, haze
			o in collect		
i	is, hit		u in focus	ch	chin, arch
ir	mirror, here			ŋ	ring, singer
ī	ice, fire	b	bed, dub	sh	she, dash
		d	did, had	th	thin, truth
o	lot, pond	f	fall, off	*th*	then, father
ō	open, go	g	get, dog	zh	s in pleasure
ô	law, horn	h	he, ahead		
oi	oil, point	j	joy, jump	′	as in (ā′b′l)
oo	look, pull	k	kill, bake		
ōō	ooze, tool	l	let, ball		
yoo	unite, cure	m	met, trim		
yōō	cute, few	n	not, ton		
ou	out, crowd	p	put, tap		

*Pronunciation key and respellings adapted from *Webster's New World Dictionary, Basic School Edition*, Copyright © 1983 by Simon & Schuster, Inc. Reprinted by permission.

A

a·board (ə bôrd′) *adverb.* on, in, or into a boat, train, airplane, or bus.

ab·so·lute·ly (ab′sə lōōt lē) *adverb.* completely; perfectly.

ac·tor (ak′tər) *noun.* a person, especially a boy or man, who performs in plays, in movies, or on television. **actors.**

ad·ven·ture (əd ven′chər) *noun.* **1.** a dangerous event. **2.** an unusual or exciting experience.

ad·vice (əd vīs′) *noun.* an opinion given about what action to take or about how to do something.

al·pha·bet (al′fə bet) *noun.* **1.** the letters of a language placed in order. **2.** a system of symbols used in communicating, such as the Braille alphabet for the blind.

am·ble (am′b′l) *verb.* **1.** to walk in a slow, easy way. **2.** to move slowly and smoothly by raising both legs on one side, then both legs on the other side; used to describe the way a horse, donkey, etc., moves. **ambled.**

an·chor (aṅ′kər) *noun.* a heavy object that is lowered into the water on a rope or chain to keep a boat from drifting, usually a metal piece with hooks that dig into the ground under the water.

an·nounce (ə nouns′) *verb.* **1.** to say or tell something to an audience. **2.** to make something known to others: He *announced* that the class would take a trip to the museum. **3.** to say or tell. **announced.**

at·ten·tion (ə ten′shən) *noun.* the ability to keep your mind or thoughts on something; notice.

awk·ward (ôk′wərd) *adjective.* **1.** not moving in a graceful way; clumsy. **2.** difficult to use or hold: It was *awkward* to carry so many packages.

ax·le (ak′s′l) *noun.* a bar or rod on which the wheels at each end turn: When the *axle* broke on the wagon, one wheel rolled down the hill.

aboard

Alphabet is taken from two Greek words *alpha* and *beta*. These two words are the names of the first two letters in the Greek alphabet.

axle

347

B

Ballet is a French word that became part of the English language. Ballet started in France three hundred years ago. When it spread to England, people used the French word for the new style of dance.

breeches

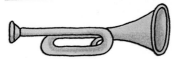

bugle

bab·ble (bab''l) *verb.* **1.** to make sounds like talking that are not understood by others; baby talk. **2.** to chatter or talk fast. **3.** to speak foolishly. —**babbling** *adjective.* bubbling or gurgling sounds, like water running over stones: The deer drank water from the *babbling* brook.

bal·let (bal'ā *or* ba lā') *noun.* a dance that tells a story through a series of planned, graceful movements usually performed by dancers wearing costumes.

beak (bēk) *noun.* **1.** the bill of a bird, especially of an eagle, a hawk, or another bird of prey. **2.** anything that looks like a bird's beak.

be·lief (bə lēf') *noun.* **1.** a thought or feeling that something is true or real; faith. **2.** anything accepted as true. **beliefs.**

blub·ber (blub'ər) *noun.* fat under the skins of seals, whales, and other sea animals.

bore (bôr) *verb.* to tire by being dull or uninteresting. —**boring** *adjective.* dull, uninteresting.

bor·row (bor'ō *or* bôr'ō) *verb.* **1.** to use something that belongs to someone else after agreeing to return it. **2.** to use someone else's ideas, ways of doing things, etc., as your own. **borrowed.**

breech·es (brich'iz) *plural noun.* short pants that stop just below the knees.

bu·gle (byōō'g'l) *noun.* a type of small trumpet, usually without playing keys or valves.

bunk (bungk) *noun.* **1.** a built-in bed that hangs on a wall like a shelf. **2.** a narrow bed: The cowboy went to his *bunk* after a hard day's work.

bunt (bunt) *verb.* to bat a baseball lightly so that it does not go beyond the infield.

busi·ness (biz'nis) *noun.* **1.** work that someone does to earn money. **2.** a place where work is done or things are made or sold. **3.** a matter or affair: The girls met to make rules and talk about other club *business.*

C

ca·ble (kā′b′l) *noun.* **1.** a strong rope, usually made of covered wires or metal twisted together. **2.** a bundle of insulated wires that conduct electricity. **3.** a shorter word for *cablegram*, a telegraph message sent overseas.

cham·ber (chām′bər) *noun.* **1.** a room, usually a bedroom. **2.** a large room used for meetings, such as an assembly hall.

charm (chärm) *noun.* **1.** something believed to have magical powers, either good or evil. **2.** a small object on a bracelet or necklace. **3.** a physical feature or a personal characteristic that is pleasing, delightful, or attractive.

chat·ter (chat′ər) *verb.* **1.** to make short, quick noises that sound like talking: The birds were *chattering* outside the window. **2.** to talk fast and foolishly without stopping. **chattering.**

chick·en (chik′ən) *noun.* **1.** a young hen or rooster. **2.** the meat of a chicken. **chickens.**

choice (chois) *noun.* **1.** the act of choosing or picking. **2.** having the chance, power, or right to choose. **3.** someone or something chosen.

choke (chōk) *verb.* **1.** to try to breathe when something is stuck in the windpipe. **2.** to squeeze the throat to stop breathing. **3.** to have trouble breathing. **choked.**

chore (chôr) *noun.* **1.** the regular light work such as that done at home or on a farm: His *chores* on the farm include feeding the chickens. **2.** a task that is difficult or uninteresting. **chores.**

clam·ber (klam′bər) *verb.* to climb by trying hard, especially using both the hands and feet: The boy *clambered* up the tree. **clambered.**

cli·mate (klī′mət) *noun.* the typical weather of a place, year after year: In some cold *climates* people wear coats all year long. **climates.**

cob·ble·stone (kob″l stōn) *noun.* a rounded stone that was used to pave the streets long ago. **cobblestones.**

a fat	oi oil	ch chin
ā ape	oo look	sh she
ä car, father	ōō tool	th thin
e ten	ou out	*th* then
er care	u up	zh leisure
ē even	ur fur	ng ring
i hit		
ir here	ə = a *in* ago	
ī bite, fire	e *in* agent	
o lot	i *in* unity	
ō go	o *in* collect	
ô law, horn	u *in* focus	

chicken

Cobblestone is made up of *cobble* and *stone. Cob* is a very old word meaning "plump" or "round."

349

Consider comes from Greek. Its meaning was "to observe the stars." Perhaps the ancient Greeks also used their star-gazing hours to think. In time, *consider* came to mean "to think things over."

crocodile

dawn

com·mu·ni·cate (kə myoō'nə kāt) *verb.* to make something known to others; to give or share information: Long ago, some Native Americans could *communicate* by sending smoke signals.

com·plain (kəm plān') *verb.* to tell about or show pain or unhappiness about something.

con·cen·trate (kon'sən trāt) *verb.* to focus all your attention on something: He will *concentrate* on learning how to play the piano.

con·sid·er (kən sid'ər) *verb.* **1.** to think about something in order to make a decision. **2.** to keep something in mind while making a decision or in taking an action. **3.** to believe something about someone. **considering.**

coun·cil (koun's'l) *noun.* **1.** a group of people who meet to make plans or decisions. **2.** a group of people elected to make the laws for a city or town.

cour·age (kur'ij) *noun.* the ability to control fear in order to go through danger, pain, or trouble; bravery.

croc·o·dile (krok'ə dīl) *noun.* a large tropical lizard like an alligator, with thick skin, a long tail, a long, narrow, triangular head with large jaws, and cone-shaped teeth.

cun·ning (kun'ing) *adjective.* clever; able to cheat or trick others: In the fairy tale, the *cunning* fox was able to fool the rabbit.

cus·to·mer (kus'tə mər) *noun.* a person who buys, often again and again, from the same place. **customers.**

D

dan·gle (dang'g'l) *verb.* to hang loosely so as to swing. **dangled.**

dawn (dôn) *verb.* **1.** to begin to be day; to grow light. **2.** to begin to happen. —*noun.* the first light of day.

deaf (def) *adjective.* **1.** not able to hear or not able to hear well. **2.** not wanting to hear or listen.

de·ci·sion (di sizh'ən) *noun.* the act of making up your mind about something, or the opinion or choice decided on: He made a *decision* to go to a different movie.

deck (dek) *noun.* **1.** the floor of a ship. **2.** a pack of 52 playing cards.

de·pend (di pend') *verb.* **1.** to trust someone to give help. **2.** to be determined by something or someone else: The amount of snowfall varies, *depending* on where you live. **depending.**

de·serve (di zurv') *verb.* to have the right to something: We worked hard and we *deserve* the prize.

des·ti·na·tion (des'tə nā'shən) *noun.* the place where someone is going.

de·ter·mined (di tur'mənd) *adjective.* **1.** having your mind made up. **2.** strong and sure.

dif·fi·cult (dif'i kəlt) *adjective.* **1.** hard to do or make; causing a lot of trouble, thought, time, or practice; hard to understand. **2.** hard to get along with.

dis·con·tent·ed (dis'kən tent'id) *adjective.* not satisfied; wanting something different.

dis·o·bey (dis ə bā') *verb.* to refuse or fail to follow orders.

dis·please (dis plēz') *verb.* to anger or dissatisfy; to be bothered by: They were *displeased* by the long lines of people outside the store. **displeased.**

dis·tance (dis'təns) *noun.* **1.** the amount of space between two points. **2.** a place far away.

dis·tress (dis tres') *verb.* to cause worry, sorrow, or trouble. —*noun.* worry; pain; unhappiness.

dive (dīv) *verb.* **1.** to plunge headfirst into water. **2.** to go underwater to look for something. **3.** to move or drop suddenly. **dived.**

dol·phin (dol'fən) *noun.* a water animal belonging to the same family as the whale, but smaller than the whale. **dolphins.**

drawn (drôn) *verb.* to be pulled: The wagon was *drawn* by two horses.

deck

E

ea·ger (ē'gər) *adjective.* wanting very much to do or get something.

ech·o (ek'ō) *noun.* a sound heard again after it bounces off a surface. —*verb.* to repeat.

dolphin

a fat	oi oil	ch chin
ā ape	oo look	sh she
ä car, father	oo tool	th thin
e ten	ou out	th then
er care	u up	zh leisure
ē even	ur fur	ng ring
i hit		
ir here	ə = a *in* ago	
ī bite, fire	e *in* agent	
o lot	i *in* unity	
ō go	o *in* collect	
ô law, horn	u *in* focus	

ed·i·tor (ed′ə tər) *noun.* a person in charge of putting together a newspaper or magazine.

ed·u·ca·tion (ej′ə kā′shən) *noun.* what you learn by being taught in school or by training.

el·e·va·tor (el′ə vāt′ər) *noun.* a platform or box that moves up and down in a shaft and that carries people and things between floors in buildings.

em·bar·rass (im ber′əs) *verb.* to make feel uncomfortable or uneasy. —**embarrassed** *adjective.* self-conscious; ashamed.

emp·ty (emp′tē) *adjective.* having nothing inside. —*verb.* to take everything out of a jar, bottle, etc.

en·gi·neer (en′jə nir′) *noun.* a person who is trained to plan and build machines, roads, bridges, etc. **engineers.**

Eng·lish (iṇg′glish) *adjective.* of England, its language, or its people.

es·pe·cial·ly (ə spesh′əl ē) *adverb.* mostly; in particular: I like candy, *especially* chocolate.

ex·it (eg′zit *or* ek′sit) *noun.* a way out of a place, such as a door. —*verb.* to go out; to leave.

> **Elevator** comes from a Latin word that means "to lighten" or "raise up."

engineer

> **Farmhand** is a compound word made up of *farm* and *hand*. *Hand* in this case refers to a person who works with his or her hands.

F

fame (fām) *noun.* known by many people through books, television, newspapers, etc.

fa·mil·iar (fə mil′yər) *adjective.* **1.** close; friendly; knowing someone or something well. **2.** acting too friendly in a pushy way. **3.** ordinary or usual.

farm·hand (färm′hand) *noun.* a person who works on a farm to earn money. **farmhands.**

fault (fôlt) *noun.* **1.** a thing or problem that keeps something or someone from being perfect. He has many *faults,* but he is still my friend. **2.** a mistake. **3.** being the cause of something unwanted. **faults.**

fa·vor·ite (fā′vər it) *noun.* a person or thing that is liked better than others. —*adjective.* best liked; preferred.

fend·er (fen′dər) *noun.* a metal piece over each wheel of a car that protects the car from mud, stones, etc. **fenders.**

fib·er·glass (fī′bər glas′) *noun.* material made of glass threads that is used to make cloth, insulation, boats, etc.

fish·er·man (fish'ər mən)
noun. someone who catches
or tries to catch fish for sport
or for a living. **fishermen.**

flake (flāk) *noun.* a small,
thin, usually flat piece of
something.

flip·per (flip'ər) *noun.* **1.** the
wide, flat body part on seals,
whales, etc., used for
swimming. **2.** a wide, flat
rubber shoe that swimmers
wear to help them move
through water. **flippers.**

flock (flok) *noun.* a group of
animals or birds that eat and
travel together.

flut·ter (flut'ər) *verb.* **1.** to
flap the wings quickly in a
short flight or without flying.
2. to move with quick
motions. **fluttered.**

fore·cast·er (fôr'kast ər) *noun.*
someone who tries to
predict how events will turn
out.

freight train (frāt trān) *noun.*
a train that carries a load of
goods. **freight trains.**

fu·ture (fyōō'chər) *noun.* a
time that is to come: In the
future, I will study more for
tests.

G

gal·ley (gal'ē) *noun.* **1.** a long,
low ship used long ago,
moved by sails and oars.
2. the kitchen of a boat or
ship: The sailor went to the
galley to start cooking.

ga·losh·es (gə losh'iz) *plural
noun.* overshoes that come
high above the ankles, worn
in wet or snowy weather.

gar·ment (gär'mənt) *noun.* a
piece of clothing, such as a
skirt, a pair of pants, etc.
garments.

glit·ter (glit'ər) *verb.* to shine
with a sparkling light.
glittered.

gloom·i·ly (glōōm'ə lē) *adverb.*
very sadly; in a deeply
unhappy way.

goal (gōl) *noun.* **1.** the
destination at the end of a
race or trip. **2.** a purpose
toward which one's actions
are aimed: Their *goal* was to
finish cleaning the house
before the guests arrived.
3. a net, line, or pocket over
or into which a ball must go
for a team or player to score
in certain games.

flock

Galoshes used to be a kind of
high wooden sandal. These
sandals were worn over shoes
to keep a person's feet out of
the mud. Today galoshes do
the same thing, but they are
made of rubber, not wood.

353

H

hes·i·tate (hez′ə tāt) *verb.* **1.** to stop or hold back for a moment as if feeling unsure. **2.** to feel unwilling to do something. **hesitated.**

hike (hīk) *noun.* a long walk, especially through the woods or in the countryside.

hon·or (on′ər) *noun.* **1.** a sign of respect: It was an *honor* to be chosen for the advanced class. **2.** credit or glory, as in winning a prize. **3.** good name.

hood

hood (hood) *noun.* **1.** a piece that covers the head and neck, often attached to a jacket or coat. **2.** a metal cover in the front of an automobile over the engine.

hoot owl (hoot oul) *noun.* a bird with a large head, large eyes, small hooked beak, and sharp claws. It makes a long, low sound.

horn (hôrn) *noun.* **1.** a musical instrument played by blowing. **2.** a device that makes a loud, warning noise.

house·hold (hous′hōld) *noun.* all the people who live in a house, especially a family.

hug (hug) *verb.* **1.** to put the arms around and hold close

hoot owl

Hoot is a good example of a word that is taken directly from a sound. The word *hoot* in *hoot owl* sounds like the call of an owl.

in a loving way. **2.** to keep close. **hugging.**

hur·ri·cane (hur′ə kān) *noun.* a storm with strong winds blowing in a circle at 73 miles per hour or more, usually with heavy rains.

I

ice·berg (īs′burg) *noun.* a huge piece of ice, floating in the sea; most of an iceberg is under the water.

i·cy (ī′sē) *adjective.* **1.** covered with ice; frozen or slippery. **2.** feeling very cold like ice.

ig·nore (ig nôr′) *verb.* to act as if something is not happening: Try to *ignore* the noises from the street and just keep talking.

in·clude (in klood′) *verb.* to take something in as a part of a whole or group: Will you *include* this in the box?

in·ning (in′ iñg) *noun.* a part of a baseball game in which both teams get a turn at bat; there are usually nine innings in a baseball game.

in·sist (in sist′) *verb.* **1.** to demand in a stubborn or strong way. **2.** to stick to an idea strongly.

in·stru·ment (in'strə mənt) *noun.* **1.** a tool or machine used to do exact work: The doctor always washed his *instruments* after he used them. **2.** something on which music can be played, such as a drum, violin, flute, etc. **instruments.**

in·ter·rupt (in tə rupt') *verb.* **1.** to make a break in something, as in someone talking: He *interrupted* the lesson when he came late to class. **2.** to keep something from going on; to cut off. **interrupted.**

in·tro·duce (in trə do͞os' *or* in trə dyo͞os') *verb.* to present or make known to others. **introduces.**

in·vi·ta·tion (in'və ta'shən) *noun.* **1.** the act of inviting a person to go somewhere or do something. **2.** the spoken or written way of inviting.

J

jun·gle (juṅg'g'l) *noun.* land in warm, moist parts of the world, covered with trees, plants, and vines.

K

key·board (kē'bôrd) *noun.* **1.** the row or rows of black and white keys on a piano or organ. **2.** the lettered and numbered keys on a computer or typewriter.

kind·ness (kīnd'nis) *noun.* the habit or way of being friendly, good, generous, etc., to others.

L

lad·en (lād"n) *adjective.* having or carrying a heavy load: Mother left the department store *laden* with packages.

lan·guage (laṅg'gwij) *noun.* **1.** the speech or writing people use to understand each other. **2.** any way of communicating thoughts or feelings, such as the way sign language uses hand gestures to mean words. **3.** the written or spoken words of a certain group of people: My pen pal speaks English as well as the Korean *language.*

a fat	ᴏɪ oil	ch chin
ā ape	o͝o look	sh she
ä car, father	o͞o tool	th thin
e ten	ou out	*th* then
er care	u up	zh leisure
ē even	ur fur	ṅg ring
i hit		
ir here	ə = a *in* ago	
ī bite, fire	e *in* agent	
o lot	i *in* unity	
ō go	o *in* collect	
ô law, horn	u *in* focus	

keyboard

laden

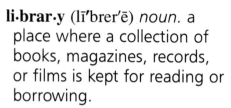

mandolin

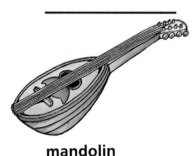

Marathon races are so named because of a messenger in Greece over two thousand years ago. This messenger ran 26 miles from a city named Marathon to the city of Athens. He delivered the message that the Greeks had defeated the Persians in battle. Modern marathons are the same distance that the ancient messenger ran.

medal

li·brar·y (lī′brer′ē) *noun.* a place where a collection of books, magazines, records, or films is kept for reading or borrowing.

lit·er·ar·y (lit′ə rer′ē) *adjective.* **1.** having to do with the written work of a country, a time in history, etc., that people enjoy reading. **2.** having to do with writing.

lull (lul) *verb.* **1.** to make or become calm or quiet. **2.** to calm by using soft sounds or movements. **lulled.**

lung (luñg) *noun.* one of the two organs in the chest used to breathe: The mountain climber took a deep breath and filled his *lungs* with fresh air. **lungs.**

M

mag·a·zine (mag ə zēn′ *or* mag′ə zēn) *noun.* a regular publication with stories, information, pictures, etc., usually coming out once each week or month. **magazines.**

main·land (mān′ land *or* mān′ lənd) *noun.* the greatest part of a country or continent; not an island.

mam·mal (mam′əl) *noun.* any of a group of animals where the females have special glands that produce milk to feed their young. **mammals.**

man·age (man′ij) *verb.* **1.** to be in charge of. **2.** to be sure that things get done in workplaces, homes, etc. **3.** to succeed in doing something: She *managed* to swim across the lake. **managed.**

man·do·lin (man′d′l in) *noun.* a musical instrument with eight or ten strings played with a pick.

man·go (mañg′gō) *noun.* **1.** a tropical fruit with a yellowish-red thick skin and a hard stone inside. **2.** the tree on which this fruit grows.

mar·a·thon (mar′ə thon) *noun.* a race run on foot, about 26 miles long.

may·or (mā′ər *or* mer) *noun.* the person elected by the people of a city or town to be in charge of its government.

med·al (med″l) *noun.* a piece of metal with words or pictures on it, usually given as a prize to people who do something special.

per·form·ance (pər fôr′məns) *noun.* the act of doing something before an audience.

per·for·mer (pər fôr′mər) *noun.* a person who acts, plays an instrument, or shows another skill before an audience. **performers.**

per·suade (pər swād′) *verb.* to get someone to act or think in a certain way by making it seem like a good thing.

pi·an·o (pē an′ō) *noun.* a large musical instrument with wire strings in a case and a keyboard.

pic·nic (pik′nik) *verb.* to go on an outing that includes eating a meal outdoors. **picnicking.**

pil·grim (pil′grəm) *noun.* **1.** a person who travels to places away from home for religious reasons. **2. Pilgrim.** one of the group of Puritans who left England and settled in Plymouth, Massachusetts, in 1620. **Pilgrims.**

pi·lot (pī′lət) *noun.* **1.** a person who steers a ship. **2.** a person who flies an airplane or helicopter.

pitch·er (pich′ər) *noun.* a baseball player who throws the ball so the batters can try to hit it.

plan·et (plan′it) *noun.* a large heavenly body that moves in an orbit or path around a star.

plow (plou) *noun.* a farm tool, pulled by an animal or a tractor, that breaks up the soil into rows to get it ready for planting.

plug (plug) *verb.* **1.** to close up a hole. **2.** to work hard and steadily at something: When we came home, the workers were still *plugging* away at digging the trench. **plugging.**

plunge (plunj) *verb.* **1.** to throw or push with great power. **2.** to dive. **plunged.**

pock·et (pok′it) *noun.* a small bag or pouch sewn into clothing and used to hold things. **pockets.**

po·em (pō′əm) *noun.* a written work that uses a pattern of sounds, tempo, and words that rhyme to show an idea or experience that is deeply felt by the writer.

po·et·ry (pō′ə trē) *noun.* **1.** the art of writing poems. **2.** poems.

po·lice·man (pə lēs′mən) *noun.* a member of the police department.

a fat	oi oil	ch chin
ā ape	oo look	sh she
ä car, father	o͞o tool	th thin
e ten	ou out	*th* then
er care	u up	zh leisure
ē even	ur fur	n̂g ring
i hit		
ir here	ə = a *in* ago	
ī bite, fire	e *in* agent	
o lot	i *in* unity	
ō go	o *in* collect	
ô law, horn	u *in* focus	

piano

Piano comes from the Italian word, *pianoforte*, which means "soft" and "strong." The inventor of the piano chose this name because the new instrument could be played both softly and loudly.

practice

punt

pop·u·lar (pop′yə lər) *adjective.* **1.** being well liked by many people. **2.** something that is liked by a lot of people.

pop·u·lar·i·ty (pop′yə lar′ə tē) *noun.* the state of being well liked.

po·si·tion (pə zish′ən) *noun.* **1.** the way a person or thing is placed. **2.** the place where a person or thing is, especially how near or far from other things. **3.** a job that someone does.

prac·tice (prak′tis) *verb.* **1.** to make a habit of doing something regularly. **2.** to repeat an action or a series of actions again and again in order to become skilled.

pre·dic·tion (pri dik′shən) *noun.* the act of trying to tell what will happen in the future.

prep·a·ra·tion (prep′ə rā′shən) *noun.* **1.** getting or being ready for something. **2.** doing things to get ready. **preparations.**

pre·pare (pri par′) *verb.* **1.** to make or get ready: He can't go with us because he has to *prepare* for a test. **2.** to make or put something together.

print (print) *verb.* **1.** to press letters or designs on to a surface. **2.** to produce writing to be sold. **3.** to write in letters similar to those in books. **printed.**

pro·vide (prə vīd′) *verb.* **1.** to give what is needed. **2.** to support. **3.** to get ready ahead of time. **provided.**

pub·lish (pub′lish) *verb.* to get a book, magazine, newspaper, etc., printed and brought to market for sale. **published.**

punt (punt) *noun.* the act of kicking a football after it is dropped from the hands but before it hits the ground.

purr (pur) *verb.* to make the soft rumbling sound a cat makes when it is happy. **purred.**

R

rack·et (rak′it) *verb.* to make a loud, clattering noise. **racketing.**

ra·di·o (rā′dē o′) *noun.* **1.** a way that sounds are sent from one place to another by changing them into electrical waves that travel through the air. **2.** a receiving set that picks up those waves and changes them back into sounds.

raw (rô) *adjective.* **1.** uncooked. **2.** in its natural state. **3.** uncomfortably cold and damp: The *raw* wind made us return home early.

re·ci·tal (ri sīt″l) *noun.* **1.** the act of telling every part of a story. **2.** a story told like this. **3.** a music or dance program where people perform on stage alone or in a small group.

re·cov·er (ri kuv′ər) *verb.* **1.** to get back something that was lost. **2.** to get well again after being sick: I am sure that she will *recover* soon from her bad cold.

re·frig·er·a·tor (ri frij′ə rāt′or) *noun.* a machine or room that keeps food, drinks, etc., cold and fresh.

re·lax (ri laks′) *verb.* **1.** to make something loose. **2.** to rest after working or doing something.

re·lief (ri lēf′) *noun.* freedom from pain, worry, or uncomfortable feelings: We were worried, but it is a *relief* to know you are safe.

re·li·gion (ri lij′ən) *noun.* **1.** a belief in God or gods. **2.** a way of living by worshipping God.

re·li·gious (re lij′əs) *adjective.* **1.** showing belief in God or a religion. **2.** having to do with religion.

re·mind (ri mīnd′) *verb.* to make or help someone remember; to tell something to someone again: He *reminded* me that we had a date. **reminded.**

re·ply (ri plī′) *verb.* to answer in words or in actions: Susan *replied* to his letter right away. **replied.**

re·ward (ri wôrd′) *noun.* **1.** something given in return for good work. **2.** money given for finding and returning something that was lost.

a fat	oi oil	ch chin
ā ape	o͝o look	sh she
ä car, father	o͞o tool	th thin
e ten	ou out	*th* then
er care	u up	zh leisure
ē even	ur fur	ŋ̆ ring
i hit		
ir here	ə = a *in* ago	
ī bite, fire	e *in* agent	
o lot	i *in* unity	
ō go	o *in* collect	
ô law, horn	u *in* focus	

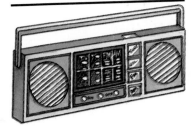

radio

S

scene (sēn) *noun.* the place and time of a play or story.

relax

361

shipwreck

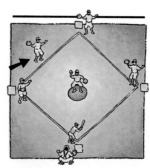
shortstop

sched·ule (skej′ool) *noun.* **1.** a list of times at which things will happen; timetable. **2.** a list of things to be done with time limits given in which those things must be done.

schol·ar (skol′ər) *noun.* **1.** a person who learns a lot by studying. **2.** a person who goes to school or studies with a teacher. **3.** a student who enjoys study and learning.

sci·en·tist (sī′ən tist) *noun.* a person who is an expert in a particular branch of science, such as biology, agriculture, etc. **scientists.**

scold (skōld) *verb.* to tell someone what he or she is doing wrong in an angry voice: He *scolded* me for arriving late for class. **scolded.**

seal (sēl) *noun.* a sea animal having four flippers that lives in cold waters and is covered with fur. **seals.**

sep·a·rate (sep′ə rāt) *verb.* **1.** to set apart. **2.** to put something between other things. **3.** to go away from one another. —**separated** *adjective.* set apart; divided.

se·ri·ous (sir′ē əs) *adjective.* **1.** having thoughts that are deeply felt; important. **2.** not joking or fooling around; sincere: John is *serious* about completing his project on time.

serv·ant (sur′vənt) *noun.* someone who is paid to work in another person's home as cook, butler, maid, etc.

shaft (shaft) *noun.* **1.** the long, thin part of an arrow or spear. **2.** a handle. **3.** one of the two long pieces of wood between which an animal pulls a wagon, plow, etc. **4.** a long tunnel dug into the earth, like a mine shaft. **5.** a long opening that goes through the floors of a building, such as for an elevator. **shafts.**

shim·mer (shim′ər) *verb.* to shine with a wavering kind of light: The puddle of water on the sidewalk was *shimmering* under the street light. **shimmering.**

ship·wreck (ship′rek) *noun.* the parts of a ship left after it is destroyed or lost at sea.

shiv·er (shiv′ər) *verb.* to shake as when you are very cold or afraid; to tremble. **shivered.**

short·stop (shôrt′stop) *noun.* a baseball player who fields the balls hit between second and third base.

sigh (sī) *noun.* a long, deep breathing sound made when sad, tired, or relieved. **sighs.**

sign (sīn) *noun.* a word, picture, or action that tells of something else. —*verb.* using a part of the body to show or mean something, as in nodding the head, waving the hand, etc. **signs.**

sign language *noun.* a system of hand gestures used to talk with people who are deaf.

slave (slāv) *noun.* **1.** a person owned by someone else. **2.** a person who is controlled by something else.

so·nar (sō′när) *noun.* a machine that sends sound waves through water, to locate objects; used to find submarines, measure the depth of the ocean, etc.

sort (sôrt) *noun.* **1.** a group of things that have something that is the same. **2.** type or kind: There are many *sorts* of toys in the store. **sorts.**

spar·kle (spär′k′l) *verb.* to shine as if giving off sparks or flashes of light.

sput·ter (sput′ər) *verb.* **1.** to spit out food or water from your mouth when speaking. **2.** to talk in a fast, excited way. **3.** to make hissing or popping noises. **sputtered.**

stage (stāj) *noun.* the raised platform in a theater on which actors and entertainers perform.

stall (stôl) *noun.* a space for one animal in a stable or barn.

stal·lion (stal′yən) *noun.* a full-grown male horse that can have offspring: The wild *stallion* galloped across the plains.

stub·born·ly (stub′ərn lē) *adverb.* in a very determined way; in a way that shows unwillingness to listen or to change one's mind: He acted *stubbornly* even after he knew he was wrong.

sub·ma·rine (sub′mə rēn) *noun.* a kind of ship that travels underwater and is able to stay there for a long time.

suf·fer (suf′ər) *verb.* **1.** to feel pain; be uncomfortable. **2.** to put up with problems, pain, worry, etc.

sug·gest (səg jest′) *verb.* to bring to mind as something to consider or think over.

sur·round·ings (sə roun′diñgz) *plural noun.* the things that are around a person or around a place: The children did their classwork in beautiful *surroundings*.

a fat	oi oil	ch chin
ā ape	oo look	sh she
ä car, father	oo tool	th thin
e ten	ou out	*th* then
er care	u up	zh leisure
ē even	ur fur	ñg ring
i hit		
ir here	ə = a *in* ago	
ī bite, fire	e *in* agent	
o lot	i *in* unity	
ō go	o *in* collect	
ô law, horn	u *in* focus	

Sonar is an acronym. An acronym is a word which is made by putting together the first letters of a longer name or description. Sonar comes from *sound navagation ranging.*

submarine

363

Television is a new word, when compared to most of the words we use. It came into use seventy years ago, when television was first being developed. The word means "seeing at a distance."

sur·vive (sər vīv′) *verb.* to stay alive under bad conditions.

sus·pi·cious (sə spish′əs) *adjective.* **1.** thinking something is wrong without knowing for sure. **2.** questioning whether you can be sure about something or someone.

T

tal·ent (tal′ənt) *noun.* a special ability that a person is born with, such as in music, math, writing, drama, etc.

tel·e·vi·sion (tel′ə vizh′ən) *noun.* **1.** a way of sending pictures from one place to another by changing them into electrical waves that travel through the air. **2.** a receiving set that picks up those waves and changes them back into light rays—pictures we can see on the set's screen.

tem·per (tem′pər) *noun.* **1.** the way you feel; mood. **2.** anger: She has quite a *temper;* she yelled at everybody.

thee (<i>th</i>ē) *pronoun.* you, as used long ago.

thrash (<i>th</i>rash) *verb.* **1.** to hit with a stick, whip, or other object. **2.** to move around wildly or without control: The fish *thrashed* around in the shallow water. **thrashed.**

throat (<i>th</i>rōt) *noun.* **1.** the front of the neck. **2.** the part of the neck through which air, food, and water pass from the mouth to the stomach or lungs.

thump (<i>th</i>ump) *noun.* **1.** a blow or hit made by something heavy. **2.** the sound made by such a blow.

thy (<i>th</i>ī) *pronoun.* your, as used long ago.

ti·tled (tīt″ld) *adjective.* **1.** having a special title such as lord, knight, lady, etc. **2.** having a title or name such as the name of a book.

tre·men·dous (tri men′dəs) *adjective.* **1.** very large or huge. **2.** surprisingly wonderful, amazing, etc.

trough (trôf) *noun.* a long rectangular container often used to feed or water animals.

V

val·or (val′ər) *noun.* courage or bravery.

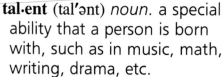

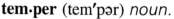

throat

trough

W

warm-blood·ed (wôrm′blud′id) *adjective.* having a body temperature that stays the same, despite the surroundings.

wasp (wosp *or* wôsp) *noun.* a flying insect, with a slender body and a narrow waist, that stings. **wasps.**

wa·ter·fall (wôt′ər fôl) *noun.* a natural stream of water that falls from a high place such as a cliff.

weap·on (wep′ən) *noun.* something used for fighting such as a club, gun, etc. **weapons.**

wea·ther vane (weth′ər vān′) *noun.* a device that turns in the wind to show which way the wind is blowing, often placed on a rooftop.

webbed (webd) *adjective.* having the toes joined by pieces of skin or flesh: Ducks have *webbed* feet.

week·ly (wēk′lē) *adjective.* happening or appearing once a week or every week.

wharf (hwôrf) *noun.* a long platform built from the shore out over the water so that ships can be loaded and unloaded.

wheel·ing (hwēl′ing) *verb.* turning around in a circular motion.

whin·ny (hwin′ē) *verb.* to make the low neighing sound that a horse makes. **whinnied.**

wig·gle (wig″l) *verb.* to twist or turn quickly from side to side. **wiggled.**

wor·ship (wur′ship) *noun.* **1.** a church service; prayer. **2.** great love or admiration of any kind. —*verb.* **1.** to offer prayers; attend church. **2.** to show great love or admiration.

worst (wurst) *adjective.* the most bad, harmful, etc.; least good.

wor·thy (wur′thē) *adjective.* **1.** having value or being wanted. **2.** being good enough for something.

writ·er (rīt′ər) *noun.* someone who writes books, essays, poems, etc., especially as a way to earn a living; author.

Y

yeowled (yould) *verb.* to yell or howl; give a loud howling cry.

yowl (youl) *verb.* to howl or cry out in a long, sad way.

a fat	oi oil	ch chin
ā ape	oo look	sh she
ä car, father	oo tool	th thin
e ten	ou out	th then
er care	u up	zh leisure
ē even	ur fur	ng ring
i hit		
ir here	ə = a *in* ago	
ī bite, fire	e *in* agent	
o lot	i *in* unity	
ō go	o *in* collect	
ô law, horn	u *in* focus	

wasp

weather vane

ABOUT THE AUTHORS

The authors listed below have written some of the selections that appear in this book. The content of the notes was determined by a survey of what readers wanted to know about authors.

EDWARD ARDIZZONE

EDWARD ARDIZZONE

Edward Ardizzone was born in Haiphong, Indochina, in what is today the country of Vietnam. When he was five years old, he moved to England with his mother and sisters. He lived in England the rest of his life. There, Edward Ardizzone became a writer and illustrator. He once described how his children's pleas for stories led him to create his books and illustrations. They would ask, "Daddy, please, please tell us a story" or "Daddy, please, draw us a picture of two elephants having a fight." It was in this way that the stories were created. Edward Ardizzone won many awards for his books, including the Kate Greenaway Medal for *Tim All Alone.* (1900–1979)

GWENDOLYN BROOKS

GWENDOLYN BROOKS

The poet Gwendolyn Brooks was born in Topeka, Kansas. She says, "I loved poetry very early and began to put rhymes together at about seven. At the age of thirteen, my poem 'Eventide' was accepted and printed in a children's magazine." When she was sixteen, she began submitting poems to a newspaper, and more than 75 of them were published. Gwendolyn Brooks won the Pulitzer Prize in poetry in 1950 for "Annie Allen." *(Born 1917)*

ANN CAMERON

ANN CAMERON

From the time Ann Cameron was in the third grade, she knew she wanted to be a writer. She says that her desire to be a writer came from her love of books. She says, "A book is something like a message in a bottle that an author throws out to sea; you never know whom it might reach, or how much it might mean to them." Ann Cameron believes that writers should write the stories they want to write: "Your story, if it's really the way you want to tell it, can never be wrong the way an arithmetic answer is wrong; and even if your mother, your father, your teacher, or your best friend doesn't understand it, it's still right for you." *(Born 1943)*

LEWIS CARROLL

LEWIS CARROLL

Lewis Carroll's real name was Charles Lutwidge Dodgson. He taught mathematics in England, but he is best known for his book *Alice's Adventures in Wonderland.* He made up the stories about Alice to tell to the children of a friend. The girls liked the stories so much they asked him to write them down. Later, he wrote another book about Alice. It is called *Through the Looking Glass. (1832–1898)*

LYDIA MARIA CHILD

LYDIA MARIA CHILD

Lydia Maria Child was born in Medford, Massachusetts. She was the youngest of six children. Her father was a baker. He made "Medford Crackers," which were very popular. He was able to give all his children a good education. Lydia Maria Child started the first U.S. magazine for children. She also wrote novels, books of games for children, and many articles against slavery. *(1802–1880)*

RAY CRUZ

Ray Cruz was born in New York City and still lives there. He studied at the High School of Art and Design, at Pratt Institute, and at Cooper Union. He has designed textiles and wallpapers and packaging for cosmetic firms. He has illustrated books for ten publishers. Ray Cruz says that he is now engaged in a personal project to illustrate a group of fairy tales in full color. *(Born 1933)*

RACHEL FIELD

Rachel Field's book *Hitty: Her First Hundred Years* won the Newbery Medal. She was the first woman to win this award. Rachel Field said she spent time writing before she did much reading. "It wasn't that I could not have read earlier. I knew the letters and all that, but it was so much more pleasant to have my mother read books to me." *(1894–1942)*

RACHEL FIELD

PAUL GALDONE

Paul Galdone is an author and illustrator of books for young people. He was born in Budapest, Hungary. He and his family moved to the United States in 1928. He had a difficult time in school because he did not speak English well. He liked biology class, however, because he could draw grasshoppers. "I was soon drawing them for all the other pupils." He has won awards for his books. He has twice been the runner-up for the Caldecott Medal. *(Born 1914)*

PAUL GALDONE

HELEN V. GRIFFITH

Helen V. Griffith says, "I have been writing and drawing since I could handle a pencil. When I was very young I wrote poetry, usually about animals. I have always liked animals, and a dog has had a featured role in many books I've written. I don't begin by thinking, 'I'm going to write about a dog,' but that's what happens." *(Born 1934)*

HELEN V. GRIFFITH

MALCOLM HALL

MALCOLM HALL

Malcolm Hall was born in Chicago, Illinois, but he grew up in Los Alamos, New Mexico. He says that the town of Los Alamos is a bit strange, because "the town itself is located on a 7000-foot mesa in the Sangre de Cristo Mountains." Both Malcolm Hall's mother and father were physicists. Malcolm Hall has written over 30 filmstrips. His book *Headlines* was a Junior Literary Guild selection. *(Born 1945)*

LEE BENNETT HOPKINS

LEE BENNETT HOPKINS

Lee Bennett Hopkins has interviewed, or talked with, many writers and illustrators. He writes about his talks with these people. He also writes poems for young people. He says, "I love doing children's books. Each one is a new challenge, a new day, a new spring for me." Lee Bennett Hopkins also puts together anthologies, or collections, of other people's poems. He goes through thousands of poems and chooses the twenty that he thinks children will enjoy most. *(Born 1938)*

JOHANNA HURWITZ

Johanna Hurwitz is a writer and illustrator of books for young people. She is also a children's librarian. She says, "My parents met in a bookstore and there has never been a moment when books were not important in my life." Johanna Hurwitz writes many letters to friends and relatives. She thinks the letter writing she does is very good training for her book writing. Her husband is also a writer. She thinks that her two children will probably be writers, too. "After all," she says, "what do you expect? Their grandparents met in a bookstore." *(Born 1937)*

JOHANNA HURWITZ

RACHEL ISADORA

Rachel Isadora writes and illustrates children's books. She is also a ballet dancer. She has been dancing since she was eleven years old. Rachel Isadora is an award-winning author. One of the awards she has won is the Boston Globe–Horn Book Award for her book *Ben's Trumpet*. Rachel Isadora's husband also writes books for young people. She has illustrated some of her husband's books, too.

RACHEL ISADORA

GENIE IVERSON

GENIE IVERSON

Genie Iverson was born in Newport News, Virginia, where her father was an officer in the Navy. She has been a reporter on a newspaper. Now she writes fables for young people as well as nonfiction. She says she writes biographies because she is interested in people and in history. *(Born 1942)*

ADA B. LITCHFIELD

ADA B. LITCHFIELD

Ada B. Litchfield grew up on Cape Cod, Massachusetts. She began writing when she was a little girl. She has published many TV scripts and books. Her TV script *Up Close and Natural* won the Ohio State Merit Award in the Natural and Physical Science Category. Ada B. Litchfield and her husband live in Stoughton, Massachusetts, with their cat Lit'l One.

PHYLLIS MCGINLEY

Phyllis McGinley wrote stories and poems for children and for adults. The first children's book she wrote was *The Horse Who Lived Upstairs*. When Phyllis McGinley wrote that book, she lived in New York City. She went to Greenwich Village to see how city horses lived. She said, "I discovered one stable that cried out for story-telling. The horses all were kept on the upper floors of the building, and they surveyed the world from their second-story windows as calmly as though they were standing in country pastures. When I noticed that their watering trough was an old cast-off bathtub, I knew I had a book." She won awards for both her poems and her stories. *(1905–1978)*

PHYLLIS McGINLEY

EVE MERRIAM

Eve Merriam has written many poems for both children and adults. She has also written books, plays, and stories. "I was writing poems when I was about seven or eight. One of my first was about a birch tree that grew outside my bedroom window. It never occurred to me that someday I might like to be a writer. I just wrote. I think one is chosen to be a poet. You write poems because you must write them; because you can't live your life without writing them." Her advice to young people who want to be writers is, "Don't be discouraged." *(Born 1916)*

EVE MERRIAM

A. A. MILNE

A. A. MILNE

Alan Alexander Milne wrote many stories and poems for children. Milne first began writing when he was seventeen. He said, "It was in the Christmas holidays of 1899 that I discovered the itch for writing which has never quite left me." He started out by writing poems. Later he began writing stories. Some of his stories are about a boy named Christopher Robin and a bear named Winnie-the-Pooh. Milne's only son was also named Christopher Robin. *(1882–1956)*

LILIAN MOORE

LILIAN MOORE

Lilian Moore was born in New York City. She writes books and poetry for young people. She has also been a schoolteacher. She taught children who had been out of school. They did not know how to read. Lilian Moore said that she was annoyed because she could not find interesting books for these children to read, so she decided to write her own books for them. She has written more than forty books since then. Some of Lilian Moore's books have been chosen as American Library Association Notable Books.

E. H. SHEPARD

E. H. SHEPARD

Ernest Howard Shepard was born in England where he lived all his life. He said that he had always intended to be an artist of some kind. Both his father and mother encouraged him in his art. He drew cartoons for the famous English magazine *Punch* for nearly fifty years. He also illustrated many books. Among the books he illustrated are *The Wind in the Willows, The Reluctant Dragon,* and *The Secret Garden.* He is probably best known for having illustrated the Christopher Robin books by A. A. Milne. He had two children. His son was killed in World War II. His daughter illustrated the Mary Poppins books. In 1972, E. H. Shepard was the recipient of the Order of the British Empire in recognition of his artistic works. *(1879–1976)*

ELIZABETH SHUB

ELIZABETH SHUB

Elizabeth Shub was born in Poland. She came to the United States when she was a child. She writes books for children and also translates books into English for other writers. She helped Isaac Bashevis Singer translate *Zlateh the Goat, and Other Stories* from Yiddish. One of her books is *Seeing Is Believing*.

JOHN STEPTOE

JOHN STEPTOE

John Steptoe is a painter and a writer and has also taught at the Brooklyn Music School. He has illustrated all of his own books as well as books for other writers. He received the Gold Medal from the Society of Illustrators for the book *Stevie*. He wrote that book when he was only sixteen years old. He says that one of the reasons he began writing books for young people was the need for "books that black children could honestly relate to." John Steptoe's new book, *Mufaro's Beautiful Daughters*, was named a Caldecott Honor Book and won the 1987 Boston Globe–Horn Book Award. *(Born 1950)*

JAMES STEVENSON

JAMES STEVENSON

James Stevenson is a writer and illustrator. Although he began his career as a cartoonist and artist, he always wanted to be a writer. He wrote magazine articles and books for adults before he began writing children's books. Now, he has written many books for young people. Several of his books have been chosen as Junior Literary Guild selections and American Library Association Notable Books. *(Born 1929)*

BRINTON TURKLE

Brinton Turkle has written and illustrated several books for children. He illustrates books for other authors, too. Brinton Turkle believes that, in a picture book, the words and the pictures should be so closely related to each other that neither one "can stand successfully alone." He says, "I feel that I have had only marginal success with this ideal, but I do keep trying and I think I am getting better." *(Born 1915)*

BRINTON TURKLE

YOSHIKO UCHIDA

Yoshiko Uchida's last name is pronounced ō chē′də. She writes books about Japan and its people and about Japanese-Americans as well. She says, "I wanted American children to become familiar with the marvelous Japanese folk tales I had heard in my childhood. I wanted them to read about Japanese children, learning to understand and respect differences in customs and culture, but realizing also that basically human beings are alike the world over, with similar joys and hopes." Some of Yoshiko Uchida's books have been selected as American Library Association Notable Books. She has also illustrated some of her own books of Japanese folk tales. *(Born 1921)*

YOSHIKO UCHIDA

JUDITH VIORST

JUDITH VIORST

Judith Viorst began writing poetry when she was seven years old. She says she wrote "terrible poems about dead dogs, mostly." She did not become a successful writer until she was grown and began writing about her own family. Now she is an award-winning author. Judith Viorst says, "Most of my children's books are for or about my own children." *(Born 1931)*

BERNARD WABER

BERNARD WABER

Bernard Waber is an author and illustrator. He has written several books about Lyle the Crocodile. Since he started writing the Lyle books, his house has become almost like a museum of crocodile things. He says there are stuffed toy crocodiles on "tables, sofas, stairs, floors, or whatever surface is available. A claw-footed bathtub—identical to the one shared at the Primm household—sits in our foyer together with its stuffed, Lyle-type occupant." Bernard Waber has won several awards for his books, including the Lewis Carroll Shelf Award.

LEONARD WEISGARD

Leonard Weisgard writes and illustrates children's books. He has won many awards for his books, including the Caldecott Medal. He says about his work, "My art studies were of value to me, but I also learned how to illustrate books by learning to dance, living, breathing, being with children, with people, being alone, reading, writing, traveling, brooding, dreaming, beachcombing, wondering, and mostly, listening to Margaret Wise Brown." He believes that an artist can find art materials in everyday things: "There is the world to choose from—clothes, bobby or cotter pins, paper clips, metal hangers, ironing boards, baking pans, and cupcake tins. Put them all together and you have an artist's studio." *(Born 1916)*

AUTHOR INDEX

COVER: Loretta Lustig
DESIGN: Design Five, NYC and Kirchoff/ Wohlberg in cooperation with Silver Brudett & Ginn

ILLUSTRATION: 4, (tl) Brinton Turkle, (tr) James Stevenson, (bl) James Stevenson; 5, (tr) James Stevenson, (bl) Roni Shephero, (br) Rachel Isadora; 6, (t) Scott Pollack, (c) Edward Ardizzone, (bl) Bernard Waber, (br) Linda Shute; 7, (tr) Paul Galdone, (cl) Edward Ardizzone; 8, (t) Ray Cruz, (br) Troy Howell; 9, (bl) Rae Ecklund, (br) Troy Howell; 10, (tl) E.H. Shepard, (tr) Bruce Degen, (b) E.H. Shepard; 11, (bl) Ashley Wolff, (bc) Bruce Degen, (br) Lane Gregory; 14–22, James Stevenson; 24–25, Wendy Edelson; 28–36, Brinton Turkle; 56–68, James Stevenson; 70–71, Roni Shephero; 72–80, Rachel Isadora; 82, (t) Carol Stutz, (bl) from *Black Beauty* by Anna Sewall, adapted by Robin McKinley, pictures by Susan Jeffers, pictures copyright © 1986 by Susan Jeffers, used with permission of the publisher, Random House, Inc., (br) illustration from *Picture Book Number 1* illustrated by Ralph Caldecott (Frederick Warne & Co.), reproduced by permission of Penguin Books Ltd.; 83, reproduced with permission of Bradbury Press, an affiliate of Macmillan, Inc., from *The Girl Who Loved Wild Horses* by Paul Goble, copyright © 1978 by Paul Goble, 84–95, Leonard Weisgard; 84, Betsy Day; 98, Susan Jaekel; 102–114, Edward Ardizzone; 120–130, Linda Shute; 134–135, Gary Torrisi; 137, Gary Torrisi; 141, Susan Jaekel; 150–158, Paul Galdone; 159, Sharron O'Neil; 160–161, Scott Pollack; 164–177, Bernard Waber; 180, Sharron O'Neil; 193, Susan Lexa; 196–204, Rae Ecklund; 206, Floyd Cooper; 211, Christa Kieffer; 212–213, Troy Howell; 214–224, Ann Strugnell; 233, Susan Jaekel; 238–245, Ray Cruz; 248, Sharron O'Neil; 252–262, Bruce Degen; 252, Bob Filipowich; 263, Sharron O'Neil; 264–265, Greg Mackey; 266–275, Larry Raymond; 276–277, (b & tr) Rich Lo; 280–281, Lane Gregory; 288–294, Les Morrill; 295, Sharron O'Neil; 296–308, John Steptoe; 312–322, Ashley Wolff; 323, Sharron O'Neil; 324–341, E.H. Shepard; 344, Susan Jaekel; 347, Diane Dawson Hearn, Claudia Sargent; 348, Roberta Holmes; 351, Deirdre Griffin; 353, Roberta Holmes; 355, Diane Dawson Hearn; 356, Deirdre Griffin, Diane Dawson Hearn; 357, Deirdre Griffin; 358, Roberta Holmes; 359, Claudia Sargent; 360, Diane Dawson Hearn; 361, Melinda Fabian; 362, Diane Dawson Hearn, Claudia Sargent; 363, Claudia Sargent; 364, Diane Dawson Hearn, Roberta Holmes.

PHOTOGRAPHY: 7, Jen & Des Bartlett/ Bruce Coleman, Inc.; 8, Laird Roberts; 12, *Snap the Whip,* Winslow Homer (American), 50.41, The Metropolitan Museum of Art, New York; 39, The Pilgrim Society, Plymouth; 40, Bettmann Archive; 41, The Pilgrim Society, Plymouth; 42, courtesy The John Hancock Mutual Life Insurance Co., Boston; 43, The Granger Collection; 99, (tl) from *And Then What Happened, Paul Revere?* by Jean Fritz, illustrated by Margot Tomes, published in 1973 by Putnam, (tr) reproduced with permission of Charles Scribner's Sons, an imprint of Macmillan Publishing Company, from *The Bears on Hemlock Mountain* by Alice Dalgliesh, illustrated by Helen Sewell, copyright © 1952 by Alice Dalgliesh, copyright renewed, (bl) from *The Farm Book,* story and pictures by E. Boyd Smith, published in 1982 by Houghton Mifflin Company, (br) from *Wagon Wheels* by Barbara Brenner, illustrated by Don Bolognese, published in 1984 by Harper & Row; 100, © Susan Van Etten; 116–117, Superstock; 133, Woods Hole Oceanographic Institute, Courtesy Sygma; 135, RONA/Bruce Coleman, Inc.; 136, Woods Hole Oceanographic Institute; 139–140, Woods Hole Oceanographic Institute; 144, Jeff Foott/Bruce Coleman, Inc.; 145, Jen & Des Bartlett/Bruce Coleman, Inc.; 146, G. L. Kooyman/Animals, Animals; 147, Jeff Foott/ Tom Stack & Associates; 148, Rod Allin/ Tom Stack & Associates; 181, (t) from *Amy Goes Fishing* by Jean Marzollo, pictures by Ann Schweninger, pictures copyright © 1980 by Ann Schweninger, reproduced by permission of the publisher, Dial Books for Young Readers, (c) reproduced by permission of Walker and Company from *A First Look at Seashells* by Millicent E. Selsam and Joyce Hunt, illustrated by Harriet Springer, published in 1983 by Walker and Company, (bl) reproduced with permission of Four Winds Press, an imprint of Macmillan Publishing Company from *Little Whale* by Ann McGovern, illustrated by John Hamberger, illustrations copyright © 1979 by John Hamberger, (br) from *Sea Songs* by Myra Cohn Livingston, paintings by Leonard Everett Fisher; 182, Boy *Juggling Shells,* Hokusai (Japanese), 14.76.59.4, The Metropolitan Museum of Art, New York; 185–190, Laird Roberts; 191, Mary Anne Facelman-Miner, The White House; 192, Laird Roberts; 206, Eduardo Patino; 209, Eduardo Patino; 226, The Granger Collection; 228, Thomas Bewick, Dover Books; 229, The Granger Collection; 231, National Portrait Gallery, Smithsonian Institution; 249, (t) reproduced

with permission of Charles Scribner's Sons, an imprint of Macmillan Publishing Company from *The Courage of Sarah Noble* by Alice Dalgliesh, illustrated by Leonard Weisgard, copyright © 1954 by Alice Dalgliesh and Leonard Weisgard, copyright renewed, (c) from *Anna, Grandpa, and the Big Storm* by Carol Stevens, illustrated by Margot Tomes, published in 1982 by Houghton Mifflin Company, (b) from *Chin Chiang and the Dragon's Dance* written and illustrated by Ian Wallace, published in 1984 by Atheneum; 250, *The Letter,* 1871, Mary Cassatt, American 1844–1926, gift of The William Emerson and Charles Henry Hayden Fund, 41.803, 10.84, Museum of Fine Arts, Boston; 276, Carlos Vergara; 277, North Wind Picture Archives; 278–279, Dan Helms/Duomo; 282, Steven Goldstein, Courtesy St. Louis Cardinals; 283, Focus on Sports; 345, (t) from *Train Whistles* by Helen Roney Sattler, illustrated by Giulio Maestro, published in 1984 by Lothrop, (cl) from *Computers* by Jane Jonas Srivastava, illustrated by James and Ruth McCrea, published in 1972 by Harper & Row, (cr) from *The Seeing Stick* by Jane Yolen, illustrated by Remy Charlip and

Demetra Maraslis, published in 1977 by Harper & Row, (b) from *Finger Rhymes* collected and illustrated by Marc Brown, copyright © 1980 by Marc Brown, reproduced by permission of the publisher, E.P. Dutton, a division of NAL Penguin, Inc.; 348, Sera Hopkins; 349, Stephen G. Maka; 350, Stephen G. Maka; 351, Leon Poindexter; 354, Carla Palau, © Frank Siteman 1988; 355, © Frank Siteman 1988; Dante Gelmetti/Bruce Coleman, Inc.; 358, Nicholas de Vore III/Bruce Coleman, Inc.; 360, © Frank Siteman 1988; 361, Mike Mazzaschi/Stock Boston; 365, C. W. Perkins/Animals, Animals; 366, Bettmann Archive/BBC Hulton; 367, (t) *Los Angeles Times,* (b) Fernando Diaz Rivera; 368, (t & b) Bettmann Archive; 369, (t) Bettmann Archive, (c) Clarion, (b) Holiday House; 370, (t) provided by author, (b) Antique Images/Putnam; 371, (t) Viking Penguin; 373, (t) The Granger Collection; 374, (t) Bettmann Archive; 376 (b) Edward E. Davis; 377, (t) Dial Dutton, Viking Penguin, (b) McElderry Books; 378, (t) Milton Viorst, (b) H.W. Wilson Co.; 379, Western Publishing.

H I J—RRD—96 95 94 93 92 91 90 89